HAUNTED ROCK & ROLL

About the Author

Matthew L. Swayne (State College, PA) is a journalist who currently works as a research writer at Penn State. He has done freelance reporting for major newspapers and other publications. This is Matt's second book. His first book, *America's Haunted Universities*, is a collection of tales about haunted colleges and universities.

GHOSTLY TALES OF MUSICAL LEGENDS

HAUNTED ROCK & ROLL

MATTHEW L. SWAYNE

Llewellyn Publications
Woodbury, Minnesota

First Edition
First Printing, 2014

Book design by Donna Burch-Brown
Cover art: iStockphoto.com/8264954/DonNichols
iStockphoto.com/15316870/PashaIgnatov
iStockphoto.com/20250408/rvbox
iStockphoto.com/15009971/BorisRabtsevich
Cover design by Kevin R. Brown
Editing by Andrea Neff

Library of Congress Cataloging-in-Publication Data
Swayne, M. L.
Haunted rock & roll : ghostly tales of musical legends / by Matthew L. Swayne. — First edition.
pages cm
Includes bibliographical references.
ISBN 978-0-7387-3923-6
1. Haunted places. 2. Rock musicians. 3. Ghosts. I. Title. II. Title: Haunted rock and roll.
BF1461.S93 2014
133.1—dc23
2013043735

Llewellyn Publications
A Division of Llewellyn Worldwide Ltd.
2143 Wooddale Drive
Woodbury, MN 55125-2989
www.llewellyn.com

Printed in the United States of America

Other Books by Matthew L. Swayne

America's Haunted Universities
(Llewellyn Publications, 2012)

Dedication

For their love of good ghost stories and great music,
I dedicate this book to my mother, Judy,
and my aunts Janet Watson and Joyce Kobuck.

In Memoriam

Caitlin A. "Kitty" Stevens
March 5, 1993–October 3, 2013

Contents

INTRODUCTION

From the moment the grinding rhythms and whip-crack backbeats of rock music first started pumping out of radio speakers and jukeboxes in the early 1950s, people instantly sensed something different, even dangerous, about this music.

You either loved it, or hated it. It moved you, or repulsed you. You either embraced it, or feared it.

Maybe it was the mysterious genesis of rock and roll that prompted this trepidation. The hardscrabble parents of rock music came from the fringes of American society: the blues-steeped Mississippi Delta and the lonesome hills of Appalachia. Both regions have one thing in common: a very real belief in the paranormal and the supernatural. In the Delta, devils walk on crossroads and voodoo priestesses cast spells on unsuspecting victims. The hill people of Appalachia know a thing or two about folk magic and spellcasting, too. Appalachian residents douse for water and seek magical remedies for maladies.

Fundamentalist preachers of that time—and of our own era—had one reason to use their pulpits to sound the warning against rock and roll. The dangers of rock and roll had nothing to do with folk magic or Southern superstition, these preachers said. Satan himself created this music as another tool to claim souls for his diabolical purposes.

Soon, rock and roll became the center of an epic debate between the forces of good and the forces of evil, or the forces of fun and the forces of boredom, depending on which side of the argument you found yourself. Fans said rock would never die; opponents prayed for its demise. This debate continues to this day.

We can debate whether it's the devil or just folk superstitions that influence rock. We can debate whether rock is a diabolical tool of the devil or just a coincidental blending of cultures and musical influences. But what is not up for debate is one indisputable fact: rock music has a paranormal history that is just as long, just as controversial, and just as mysterious as the musical history of rock and roll.

In the pages ahead, we'll find that the tales of the bizarre and stories of the weird fill every paranormal category, from rock and roll ghost stories to the wild tales of synchronicity that touched some of rock's most famous celebrities.

The ghost stories began almost as soon as the new music began to heat up the airwaves, and they continue to this day. We'll find that we can see, hear, and even smell these spirits in the mansions that rock stars once owned and in the graves where they now rest. You'll also read stories of blood-curdling screams that still echo, like broken gold records, over crash sites and tales of the restless spirits of rock's grande dames who refuse to take that last encore. You'll find that rock ghosts still hang out in haunted concert halls and studios as well as spirit-filled rock clubs.

We'll explore the mysterious omens and premonitions that predicted everything from instant fame to sudden death. We'll investigate the power of numbers to foretell deadly events and consider the poor timing of a prediction that failed to prevent rock's greatest tragedy.

Finally, we'll learn that ghosts aren't the only things that follow rock musicians; there are curses that seem to haunt rock's biggest names. Rock historians point to the strings of misfortune and examples of bad timing to prove the existence of rock curses. There's even a club for rock stars who have their mortal expiration date set at twenty-seven years of age.

So, it's time to plug in, tune up, raise the curtain, and take our first step on the long, winding, and haunted road of rock and roll's paranormal legacy as we pay a visit to rock stars who, like the music itself, never die.

SECTION I

ROCK STAR GHOSTS

After more than a half century, we can finally and officially say that rock and roll was never just a fad. It was more than a temporary youth-buoyed cultural movement that was destined to die out when the tidal wave of baby boomers who filled the concert halls and enlisted in fan clubs got older—and more responsible.

Rock was more than a dance craze. The jitterbug and the Charleston came and went. But, much to the consternation of parents everywhere, rock's new dance steps, like the twist and the stroll, seemed to spontaneously combust and spread throughout the country. While those dances eventually burned out, the music did not.

As it turned out, the kids were right: rock and roll didn't die, and it is not only still with us, but has matured into an artform, right up there with jazz and classical music. Teen idols, like Elvis and the Beatles, became genuine icons. Rock concerts went from primitive affairs—just a couple guys and a set of drums—to elaborate productions. The audience transformed from screaming teenyboppers to rapt, near-religious congregations of the faithful.

What no one could have predicted was that rock and roll—which celebrated youth and life as no other cultural movement did before it—would become one of America's most haunted artforms.

In the past six decades or so, rock and roll has been welded into our global psyche, producing more than just songs and guitar riffs. This short, turbulent history also created its own mythology, complete with rock gods and devils, angels and demons. The mythology is filled with rock stars grabbing sudden fame and suffering equally swift downfalls. They lived tragic lives and died heroic deaths.

Folklorists suggest that this type of passion and intrigue easily translates into legends and ghostlore. Ghostlore is a type of folklore about ghosts and spirits. Think of it as a collection of after-life urban legends. One example of rock and roll ghostlore is the classic tale of a long-dead rock legend appearing to a budding musician to help him or her gain courage and inspiration as the musician faces a critical career decision or prepares for a milestone performance.

Many folklorists don't believe in ghosts, but they do believe that rock ghostlore stands as an interesting cultural artifact, something that hints at the power of music and art to transform our culture. You may decide to categorize some of the stories ahead as nothing more than ghostlore, fun tales about our favorite celebrities.

But is there something more? There's a shady line that separates the world of the living from the world of archetypes and myth. It's called the spirit world, and rock stars are all too familiar with that thin line. The lifespan of a rock star is notoriously short. Some say that rock stars have the most dangerous occupation in the world, with all due respect to undersea welders and Alaskan crab fishermen.

Paranormal researchers say that people who are taken from this earth too soon find it hard to transition from life to death. Some of the most famous rock and rollers were taken suddenly and tragically, the victims of car accidents and plane crashes. Others, who fell under the spell of rock's notorious excesses, played a part in their own demise, succumbing to alcohol overindulgence and drug abuse.

Rockers who live by the motto "Live fast, die young, and leave a good-looking corpse" may want to add one more thing to this list. It might work better as "Live fast, die young, leave a good-looking corpse, and become a restless spirit."

Researchers also believe that the big personalities and the love of the spotlight may turn rock stars into rock ghosts. These experts say that if you watch any concert, the musicians give off a tremendous amount of energy. That psychic energy radiates through the audience, which responds. This energy may stay on long after the celebrity has passed.

They also report that since rock stars typically love their job, they may see no reason to break on through to the other side, as Jim Morrison put it.

In this section, we'll visit the sites where rock stars never die and hear reports of places where these rockers keep on rolling.

We'll travel to Iowa, where the moon sprays silver light on the neat squares of fields near Clear Lake, a town surrounded by grain bins, fences, farms—and ghosts. Only the wind whispers in this solemn and quiet corner of America's heartland. At least on most nights. On other nights people say they can hear screams and the crash of metal twisting, along with the howls and gusts of the breezes racing along the forgotten fields.

The 1960s were bad years for the live-hard, die-young set of rockers, many of whom died just as they were making their mark on the music scene. But the decade was a great era for ghosts. Several of the biggest stars of the 1960s have left their paranormal mark.

Don't think that rock and roll ghost stories ended in the 1960s, though. We'll investigate tales of dead rock legends and departed pop divas who are still seen by friends, family members, and fans. Some are as recent as yesterday's headlines, including a few star-crossed divas and a pioneer in grunge, a punk-influenced type of music that dominated the airwaves in the 1990s.

When rock stars were finally finished rampaging across the globe on their world tours, they retired to mansions—and even castles. From Tennessee to Loch Ness, homes that belonged to rock stars are considered some the world's most haunted parcels of real estate.

We'll visit those sites, too.

Our first stop, though, is a trip into the swampy bogs and down the mean streets that gave birth to rock and roll. The guitar slingers and gravelly-voiced singers from the Deep South and from America's bleak urban landscapes brought us the blues, the artform that would later morph into rock and roll and serve as a fine occult foundation for rock's greatest paranormal accounts. That's where we'll start out journey: in the cradle of the blues, a place where tales of a mysterious death and a devilish legend of a bluesman wait for us—at the crossroads.

CHAPTER 1

ROBERT JOHNSON:

Of Hellhounds and the Devil at the Crossroads

Sorry, Elvis. No offense, Mozart. But Robert Johnson is the first rock star.

Johnson may also be rock's first ghost—or, at least, he may be the subject of rock and roll's first great ghost story.

It's true that most rock historians will tell you that rock started with Johnson. The modern guitar hero who wails away on his Fender Stratocaster or sunburst Gibson Les Paul would not exist if it wasn't for a mysterious Delta bluesman named Robert Johnson. Nor would rock and roll exist—apparently—if it wasn't for Johnson's guitar mentor: the devil.

Little is known about the early life and career of Robert Johnson, whom critics and historians call "the Grandfather of Rock and Roll." What is even more frustrating for musicologists is that the facts about Johnson are so blended into the legend and rumor that it's hard to tell where Robert Johnson the man ends and where Robert Johnson the myth begins.

But that's typical for the Mississippi Delta region, a boiling cauldron of myth and mystery.

Emerging out of this bubbling froth of mystery are the somewhat accepted details that Johnson was born in Hazlehurst, Mississippi, in either 1911 or 1912. Most blues aficionados believe that he was born to Julia Dodds and Noah Johnson. His mother, however, was married to Charles Dodds, a well-off landowner and furniture maker who was, the story goes, forced off his property by a mob of whites after he dared to test the land rights of some white landowners.

Early reports say that as a young man, Johnson enjoyed music, or maybe he enjoyed looking at the dozens of pretty women who circled the great bluesmen who played it. Whether it was the actual music or the ladies that attracted him, Johnson quickly discovered he had a slight problem. He never showed much proficiency at guitar. In fact, the people who heard him play said he was only a mediocre guitar player (and others said that this assessment was a bit too generous).

Undeterred, Johnson practiced and practiced, growing more desperate to learn blues guitar. He admired the smooth guitar players who traveled the circuit of bars and juke joints in the South, guys like Eddie James "Son" House, one of the premier bluesmen of the day.

Who could blame Johnson? There were few opportunities for a black man in the Deep South at the turn of the twentieth century. He could pick cotton, or pick guitar. For a talented guitarist, playing the blues was a way out of the brutal life of a sharecropper or farm laborer. The money, booze, and good times flowed relatively freely at juke joints—those bars and clubs that dotted the Delta landscape—for guys who could play the blues. But even that path wasn't assured. Crowds knew what they wanted, and you either had it or you didn't. If you didn't, it was back to the farms and back to soul-breaking work sweating under the merciless Mississippi sun.

Johnson, the young wannabe guitarist, made no secret that he admired something else about the blues performers who crossed his path: their ability to attract women who seemed to hang on to every lyric and every note that came from them. The blues, it seems, may not have just given rise to rock and roll; it gave rise to rock and roll groupies.

Son House, who was already a respected bluesman when Johnson was just starting, said he tried to help the upstart, but teaching the kid was hopeless. He was terrible. He didn't know a guitar lick from a lick of sense.

Other sources said Son was not quite the benevolent blues guitar instructor. Rather than politely declining to help Johnson, House ridiculed Johnson at some crowded juke joint. He told Johnson that he just didn't have "it." Johnson created more racket than music on his guitar, Son said, and he just did not have that indefinable spirit that unites musician with instrument, the spirit that makes blues music the authentic artform that it is.

The scolding from one of the great names in blues history may have been enough to scare the devil out of some players, but it seemed to scare the devil right into Johnson. No matter how bad the verbal berating was, the musicians had to hand it to Johnson: he was determined to either find someone to teach him the blues, or go to hell trying.

They may have admired Johnson's heart, but they weren't about to waste their time trying to teach those clumsy hands how to play. The best musicians pretty much left him alone, or ducked behind the nearest wall or building, when they saw the hungry, lanky, unteachable guitar player coming down the street.

It is not known whether Johnson realized that the blues players had given up and exiled him from their inner circle. What is known is that Johnson seemed to exile himself. One day, however, Johnson up and left. He just disappeared. No one heard why he was leaving. No one knew his destination. And, quite frankly, no one cared. Johnson had a reputation for being nice—but a little on the weird side.

According to Samuel Charters' biography on the guitar legend, Shines, a fellow blues musician and a buddy of Johnson's, described his friend: "Robert was a very friendly person, even though he was sulky at times, you know. And I hung around Robert for quite a while. One evening he disappeared. He was kind of a peculiar fellow."

The guitar players whom Johnson badgered for lessons must have let out a huge sigh of relief that could have been heard across the Delta when they realized the nice but talentless bluesman was gone. Johnson wasn't a blues has-been; he was a blues never-was.

At least that's what they thought.

About a year or so later, Johnson showed up again in the Delta. Well, the fella looked like Robert Johnson. But when this familiar stranger started to strum and pick his guitar, it sure didn't sound like Robert Johnson. In those short 365 days, Robert had mastered the most complicated blues riffs—and even created his own intricate variations. His speed and accuracy produced dazzling licks that put the old veterans to shame.

He must have found one hell of a teacher, the musicians whispered when they heard him play, "hell" being the operable term. When Johnson started to strum and stretch, pick and pound that guitar, listeners said he played like a demon possessed. And they weren't necessarily trying to use an analogy.

People sensed something odd—even evil—about this turn of events. The rumor quickly spread that Johnson never could have picked up this skill in such a short time. He must have sold his soul to the devil. There was a common myth in the Deep South that if you wanted something bad enough, the devil just might pay you a visit with an offer. All you needed for collateral was a soul.

Another strange rumor swirled around the sudden talents of this guitar player. Some people said that late at night, Johnson would play his guitar in graveyards. It wasn't much of a stretch to guess that it wasn't good acoustics that Johnson was seeking out among the tombstones and mausoleums; the people believed this bluesman was on friendly terms with the spirits and demons that were said to hang out in those courtyards of the dead.

One thing people agreed on was that Johnson was just the type of guy to take such a deal. He was desperate to become a blues guitarist. He was desperate to make some money. He was desperate to have the fawning attention of the women who crowded into juke joints to watch their stars. Everyone could see Johnson's signature on the dotted line of a contract with the devil.

Johnson did nothing to dispel these rumors. He even said, during a drinking session, that he met the devil at the crossroads and pledged his soul if the devil could give him the power to be a great guitar player. As proof, Johnson gave the exact location of where the transaction took place. Some say Johnson met the devil at the crossroad near the Dockery Plantation one midnight. The Dockery Plantation, located between Ruleville and Cleveland, Mississippi, is one of the places considered to be the home of the Delta blues. It's also regarded as a metaphysical auction house, with the devil being one of the main bidders.

According to the legend, Johnson traveled to the crossroads, guitar in hand, when he met up with Satan. Satan told Johnson he would give him the power to play guitar like a master; he just wanted his soul as payment. To raise the stakes, Satan said he wouldn't just be a good guitar player; good guitar players were a dime a dozen in the South. No, Satan promised that Johnson would be the King of the Delta Blues.

Johnson agreed.

He traveled back to Mississippi and relished the shocked looks on the faces of the bluesmen as he tore into licks that even they couldn't master. Maybe it was jealousy, or maybe it was the deep current of Christian beliefs that penetrated the soul of even the most hard-drinking, hard-living Southern bluesman, but the musicians started to pry into Johnson's secret.

You didn't have to look far to find signs of the pact with the devil. Johnson's lyrics are full of Satanic imagery; he mentions Satan in at least six of his songs and even describes an encounter with his Satanic Majesty in one song that sounds eerily similar to the rumors that were spreading around the South about this wickedly talented guitar player.

He sang about walking with the devil in "Me and the Devil Blues." In another song, recorded in his last-ever session, Johnson prophesied that his deal was about to be closed—and it wouldn't be a pretty end. In "Hellhound on my Trail" he sang about being followed by an evil spirit, a hellhound.

Johnson wasn't the first blues musician to talk about hellhounds. His contemporaries and blues artists before him spoke about evil beings and bad luck that haunted their lives. They called them hellhounds. But most of the good citizens of Mississippi didn't need to guess what type of hellhound was on Johnson's trail: it was Satan and he was coming to collect on a debt.

The hellhound finally caught up to Johnson near Greenwood, Mississippi, in 1938. Some say he drank too much whiskey after a series of gigs at a dance hall and died. Others say maybe Robert drank too much, but it was his messing around with another man's woman that did him in. According to this story, Robert was fooling around with the girlfriend—or wife—of the owner of a juke joint. The jealous lover decided to take care of Johnson once and for all and put poison—some say strychnine—in Johnson's whiskey bottle when he wasn't looking.

There was one more explanation for the bluesman's sudden and horrific demise: maybe the devil finally collected his final payment on the contract. After all, Johnson was reportedly twenty-seven when he died. As we'll discover, it seems that a lot of contracts expire for rock stars at age twenty-seven. Rock historians say that Johnson was the first member of the notorious "27 Club," which we'll talk more about in an upcoming chapter.

All of this is speculation, though. Whatever the actual cause, the guitarist fell ill. The illness lasted for days—and the suffering was terrible. He finally died on August 16, 1938.

Now, it's not just Johnson's mystical licks and blues-bending notes that haunt the crossroads of the Delta; the ghost of Johnson, himself, has been said to show up.

How he appears differs in the tales told by people who claim they have had a ghostly encounter with the blues master. He's a shadow flitting right at the edge of darkness in some tales. Others say the ghost of an unhappy man is seen at the crossroads where Johnson made his deal. The spirit usually shows up at midnight.

Still more reports come from other sites made famous by the Johnson legend. His gravesites are hotspots for blues enthusiasts and ghost hunters. And, by the way, "gravesites" is accurate. Like everything in Johnson's life, his final resting spot is cloaked in mystery. Perhaps to confuse the devil who was coming to collect on Johnson's debt, his friends and family buried Johnson's body in one of three different spots. One is near Greenwood, Mississippi. Another is in Quito, Mississippi. A third gravesite has been located north of Morgan City, Mississippi.

These gravesites are favorites of ghost hunters seeking EVPs—electronic voice phenomena. Many claim you can still capture a little of that blues spirit walking around the area.

But, more often than not, the spirit of Robert Johnson is not captured on ghost-hunting equipment or caught on a recording device. His spirit isn't even the typical apparition of a wispy, fleeting form of a person. The spirit of Robert Johnson is much more subtle. When you're at the crossroads, or near his grave, ghost hunters say you get a feeling, like someone is watching and waiting.

Someone with a contract in hand.

CHAPTER 2

ELVIS PRESLEY:

The King Refuses to Leave the Building

If the devil hangs out waiting for musicians at the crossroads, then he must spend a lot of time in Memphis, Tennessee.

Memphis, situated on the banks of the Mississippi River, is a geographic and cultural crossroads. Here, bluegrass and blues mix with gospel and country music. Rockabilly mixes with swing music.

This is the crossroads city where rock and roll was born.

The city is also seen as a bridge between white and black cultures. Steeped in a stew of Christian beliefs, Southern folkways, and traditional African religions, Memphis is a melting pot of supernatural beliefs. From bizarre creatures that haunt cemeteries to ghost-infested Southern mansions, there are more than a few places to touch the paranormal in the River City.

Right downtown, you'll find Earnestine and Hazel's. Glowing with neon lights and the world-famous "Soul Burger" window sign, it's not just a musical hotspot, it's a haunted hotspot. The bar's rich history, while a mere thread in the haunted tapestry of the city, has primed this place for paranormal activity. We'll talk a little more about the ghosts that rock Earnestine and Hazel's in an upcoming chapter.

But most people who come to Memphis are trying to find the spirit of a kid from Memphis who rocked the world with a sneer, a hip swivel, and a voice that defined a new sound that would later be dubbed rock and roll.

If you're touring Memphis searching for signs of Elvis's spirit or just looking for a slice of the city's smoking nightlife, you must visit Beale Street. It turns out that Beale Street is a hotspot for both Memphis nightlife and its afterlife nightlife. Beale Street—the same street where Elvis bought his clothes and where he discovered the power of the blues—is the epicenter for the paranormal in the city.

The whole place is steeped in the spirit of Elvis, but his presence is particularly felt on this famous street, which was the hopping heart of Memphis back in the King of Rock and Roll's day and is still populated with bars and music clubs. As you walk down Beale, you won't be the first tourist to catch sight of a lanky young man with well-coiffed jet-black hair ducking into the shadows of the street.

He's not the only spirit that you might run into.

Another one of the city's favorite ghosts, whom most people call "Mary," resides on Beale Street, which, on any given night, fairly rocks with soul, blues, and, of course, rock and roll. You'll find Mary at the Orpheum Theatre, which sits at the corner of South Main and Beale, in this raucous section of town.

Mary reportedly responds to music that is played at the theater. Her activity increases when she hears certain tunes. It shouldn't be a surprise. In a town that once was home to a whole wing of Rock and Roll Hall of Fame inductees—people like Johnny Cash and Carl Perkins—Mary, like a lot of Memphis residents, just loves music. And in this kingdom of spirits and music, the haunted castle of Memphis's musical royalty is Graceland.

Graceland was originally owned by newspaper publisher S. E. Toof. Toof gave the estate its peaceful name in honor of his daughter, Grace, who eventually inherited the mansion and grounds.

In 1957, Elvis, whose burgeoning star status was causing security and privacy concerns, made the move to Graceland. Following Elvis's death (that is, if you believe he actually died), Graceland became the setting for several haunted encounters. Paranormal researchers believe that the haunting is caused, primarily, by the strong personalities who lived and worked in Graceland. Of course, Elvis was undoubtedly the mansion's biggest personality. But Elvis's mom, Gladys Presley, was a big personality, too. She lived in Graceland and, some say, she still walks through the mansion's halls and lush grounds.

Gladys and Elvis had a special bond. In fact, you could almost say they had a psychic connection. Gladys was protective of her son, and when she passed away, staff members say that her spirit remained to keep an eye on Elvis. Witnesses said that they saw an apparition who looked a lot like Gladys on several occasions in the mansion.

In one story, Minnie Mae, or Dodger, which is the nickname Elvis gave his grandmother, said she heard strange noises coming from the mansion's vast attic shortly after Gladys's death. She believed it was Gladys.

The stories of the haunted attic circulated among the family members, eventually reaching Priscilla, Elvis's young bride. She didn't believe in ghosts, but one night as a storm raged outside, she was determined to solve this family mystery once and for all. She made her way to the attic. It was pitch black. Priscilla struggled to find a light. When she did, a dull bulb revealed a line of clothes and dresses owned by her departed mother-in-law. She believed that Gladys had led her to the attic and sensed her joy. Priscilla tried on a few of the clothes and hats.

That's when it happened.

Priscilla said she actually felt Gladys hug her. That embrace was the only connection Priscilla had with Elvis's mom, but she reported that it was a powerful moment for her.

Like Mother, Like Son

Gladys is forever joined with Elvis at Graceland. Her grave rests next to that of her beloved little boy in a small grove on the grounds of Graceland called Meditation Garden.

Gladys is seen as more than a sage dispenser of motherly advice by Elvis biographers. She was his early spiritual adviser, too. Most biographers say that Elvis was introduced to the supernatural through the stories of his mother. Her spiritual influence lasted throughout Elvis's lifetime. He became a student of the mystical and the supernatural. He was an avid reader of a wide range of metaphysical subjects, and the King's friends said he was almost obsessed with the spirit world.

While often portrayed as a bit of a bumpkin by the press, Elvis was undeniably honest in his search for a spiritual reality behind the world of appearances.

The Christian Science Monitor reported that Elvis used to say, "Truth is like the sun. You can shut it out for a time, but it ain't goin' away."

Biographers often say that the stories Gladys spun about Elvis's birth may have initiated this lifelong quest to understand the supernatural. The King was actually an identical twin. His twin, named Jesse Garon, was stillborn. For Elvis, the name alone, which sounded so much like his own full name, Elvis Aaron (or Aron), must have reminded him that a bridge existed between the world of the living and the spirit world. Elvis always said he felt like he was missing a piece of himself and was known to "talk" to Jesse, this missing half.

It was his first connection to the spirit world, but not his last.

When Elvis passed away on August 16, 1977, Elvis fans—and the country, in general—went into a state of shock. The biggest star in the rock and roll universe—and the star whom many Americans had grown up with—was extinguished.

The light may have gone out. The music may have faded. But the spirit of Elvis rocked on. Stories of the King's ghost refusing to leave the stage appeared throughout the country.

One of the first sightings was at that small family cemetery at Graceland that contains the graves of Elvis; his parents, Gladys and Vernon; and his beloved grandmother, Minnie Mae, aka Dodger. (A marker also memorializes Elvis's stillborn brother, Jesse Garon.) Several accounts detail mysterious forms that have appeared near Meditation Garden, as Elvis named the plot.

People have seen forms wander through the small plot. Visitors have also reported seeing strange occurrences of electromagnetic interference, or orbs, when they attempt to take pictures and document their tour with video cameras and camera phones. Orbs—well known and hotly debated in the paranormal field—show up in photographs and are often shaped like faces. These filmy globs of light can also flash out of nowhere on video footage. Some say these manifestations indicate the presence of ghosts, while others say they're just dust, bugs, or electromagnetic anomalies.

One of the bizarre aftershocks of the collective quake of grief that erupted after the death of Elvis Presley was the rash of Elvis sightings that occurred throughout the country—and even the world. People claimed to see Elvis working at gas stations and eating at Burger Kings.

Most suspected that Elvis was still alive. He became bored and disillusioned by fame and wanted a break, so he decided to fake his own death. Or so the story went. Believers offered evidence: the inconsistency between the birth certificate and the spelling of Aaron on the gravestone. (On the King's birth certificate, Aaron is spelled with only one *A*: Aron.) Of course, the eyewitness sightings of Elvis enjoying a Whopper at a Burger King in Little Rock, Arkansas, cemented the theory.

But paranormal experts suggest another reason for these Elvis sightings: it's not the corporeal body of a disgruntled King of Rock and Roll that people are seeing, it's his spirit.

The Haunted America Tours site has a story about an interesting run-in with (possibly) the King. The business offers ghost tours of several haunted places around the United States.

According to this account, a mother and her husband and young daughter decided to go to Graceland. While Mom wasn't exactly an Elvis fan, the trip to the King's home sounded fun—and when you're in Memphis, a visit to Graceland is almost required. Plus, the woman had some odd connections with Elvis. Her cousin, she said, lived in Memphis and was actually working at Baptist Memorial Hospital when Elvis died there.

In any event, the tour was going well. At one point, they found themselves in the Trophy Room, where many of Elvis's costumes and awards are on display. Most people will tell you that this part of the tour is a highlight (although the Jungle Room runs a close second). As the family viewed the walls of gold records, trophies, and awards, the daughter was right by her mother's side. Suddenly, however, one of those typical motherly intuitions that something was wrong struck the woman. She looked around and her daughter was gone. Vanished.

The daughter had been there just a second earlier, so she couldn't have gone far. But it was almost as if she had disappeared into thin air. Panic set in, especially after the parents checked around the corners and saw absolutely no sign of the lost girl.

The mother, of course, alerted the tour guide, who made sure all the doors were closed. They were afraid she had been abducted, and instantly went into action.

Eventually, the search party found the girl, but she was nowhere near the Trophy Room. Instead, she was found near Elvis's grave in the Meditation Garden. When the parents and a team of rescuers ran to her, the daughter was calmly playing and talking to herself. They asked her what happened, and the story became another exhibit in Graceland's own haunted Trophy Room.

She said that a "very nice man" in a white suit had taken her by the hand and given her a quick tour of the mansion. He dropped her off by the monument—and then he "disappeared." There was no one on the tour wearing a white suit, by the way.

That happened years ago, and the daughter is now an adult. The mother, though, is still curious and once asked her daughter if she remembered the incident, but unfortunately she had no recollection of her angelic tour guide that afternoon.

Still, the ghost story does fit Elvis Presley's supernatural profile. He loved kids. He loved to help people. It sounds exactly like what Elvis would do if he came along a little lost girl at Graceland. He would calm her down, take her on a little tour, and drop her off somewhere safe.

According to *Hauntings and Horrors*, a book about haunted sites in the United States, there's another ghost story about Elvis. This time, however, he's not leading a tour, but is giving directions. In this tale, a truck driver picked up a hitchhiker on a road near Memphis. When the driver asked the stranger's name, he replied that he was Elvis Presley. At first, the driver was incredulous. Maybe the hitchhiker was a little deranged. But he looked a little, and talked a lot, like the departed King.

The truck driver followed the man's directions to his home: Graceland.

Skeptics will note that "haunted hitchhiker" stories are common bits of ghostlore. But still, it makes you wonder, especially when the report is taken in with all the other snippets of ghostly run-ins with Elvis.

There have been more spirit sightings right on the Graceland grounds, including a famous appearance at the mansion's pool house. The story goes like this. During a tour, a few visitors broke away from the main group and saw a man in the pool house, which is located on the grounds of the Graceland estate. The man looked exactly like Elvis, even though the tour took place four months after Elvis's death. If he was an Elvis impersonator, he sure got a jump on the competition.

At the time, however, most people who heard about the sighting at the pool house did not assume it was a ghost. Most conspiracy experts came to the conclusion that Elvis faked his own death and that the man in the pool house was, indeed, Elvis.

Later, though, as the conspiracy theories began to fade, people came to a more supernatural conclusion: this was the ghost of Elvis. In fact, they go even further with this theory. They believe that the dozens of Elvis sightings around the country might not be simply a depressed King of Rock and Roll looking for some kicks or even an Elvis look-alike; it's Elvis's spirit traveling to his old haunts.

And there does seem to be evidence that the King is making his presence known in one of his favorite spots: Las Vegas.

Viva Las Vegas

Elvis loved everything about Las Vegas during his life, so it's no surprise that a hunk of the King stayed there after his death. His spirit has been spotted all over the gambling mecca, including a few of Sin City's most famous hotels.

The Las Vegas Hilton is one of the prime venues where you can find the spirit of Elvis. Some of Presley's most famous shows of his later career occurred at the Hilton. These shows defined the white-sequined, glitzy, and sort of schmaltzy King of Rock and Roll. In 1969, Elvis performed a string of sold-out shows that broke all Vegas attendance records at that time. When he performed there, the hotel's owners set him up in the posh penthouse suite—room 3000 on the thirtieth floor.

No wonder he doesn't want to leave.

Although you could say that Elvis's Viva Las Vegas spirit can be felt everywhere in the city, his presence has definitely been felt in the penthouse of the Hilton and detected in other places in the hotel. Stagehands, for instance, report that they've seen that white-sequined, jumpsuit-wearing Elvis strolling backstage and preparing for one more show. Reports regularly come in of employees who take a quick glance at the stage elevator and swear they see a figure of a person who looks like Elvis. By the time they complete their double take, he's gone.

Workers and visitors at the Heartbreak Hotel, named after Elvis's iconic breakthrough hit, claim that he still makes regular appearances at the hotel, too. The lobby seems to be particularly haunted. Some people even report that they can hear him singing in the wedding chapel. Others say they captured the ghostly image of someone who looks exactly like

Elvis in pictures, even though there was nobody in the shot when they snapped the photo.

Nashville Dreams

As a child, Elvis dreamed of making it big in Nashville. He dreamed of performing on stage at the Ryman Auditorium, which played host to the *Grand Ole Opry*, a radio show that Elvis and his family listened to religiously. Elvis knew that appearing on the *Grand Ole Opry* would make his mama so proud.

But those hopes and dreams were dashed when Elvis, as a rising young regional celebrity, auditioned for the show. The tryout is seen as a pivotal moment in the Presley legend. Biographers say that when Elvis appeared in front of the judges at the Ryman, he didn't look like anything the *Grand Ole Opry* talent scouts had seen before. In fact, he wasn't like anything the city of Nashville had seen before. Pimped out in his flashy Beale Street duds and unable to control his swiveling hips, Elvis rolled through the two songs cruising up the Memphis charts: "That's All Right" and "Blue Moon of Kentucky."

The judges were not impressed.

After being turned down curtly by the judges, Elvis asked for one more chance. The judge retorted, firing a shot that was heard round the world:

"Why don't you go back to driving that truck, son."

But Elvis didn't go back to Memphis, ducktail between his legs, and he didn't take the judge's advice to quit music and pursue his truck-driving career. He went back and became the biggest international star of all time.

Ah, revenge can be sweet.

There are some, though, who say Elvis never got over that sting of rejection—and that may be a reason why his spirit is still haunting Nashville. It may be the reason why he's still hanging around the Ryman, too, according to a report that was leaked by a member of the entourage of Lisa Marie Presley, Elvis's beloved daughter. Lisa Marie, who had a bit of a music career herself, was in the Ryman for a performance. After the show, she went backstage to her dressing room.

When she tried to open the door, it was locked. Well, it wasn't locked exactly. It felt more like it was being held shut by some force.

Lisa Marie's bodyguard took over—and he was a big dude. He didn't have any success either. He called the other bodyguard, and the gigantic duo gave the door another shove. And another shove. And another.

Sometimes the door would open briefly, but would just as quickly slam shut again.

Exasperated, the group called out to whoever was holding the door to stop messing around, or they would call the cops.

A strange laugh echoed in the room. Some members of the entourage had worked with both Lisa Marie and her father, and they immediately recognized that mischievous laugh right away. It was the King's.

Another area that's frequented in Nashville by the spirit of Elvis is Music Row, the city's legendary street of big hopes and busted dreams.

Music Row is a section of the city located just southwest of downtown Nashville and houses recording studios, record company offices, music publishers, radio stations, and the ghost of Elvis Presley.

Elvis recorded in RCA's legendary Studio B. He changed the course of music history when he recorded "Heartbreak Hotel" in the studio.

But the folks who still work in the building are careful not to mention the name Elvis. It seems that odd things happen anytime the name is uttered. Once, after a worker started talking about Elvis, a ladder crashed down. Fortunately, no one was hurt, according to reports. In another incident, someone mentioned Elvis and the studio speakers erupted in an odd droning noise. After a lengthy but fruitless search, the engineers gave up trying to determine the origin of the weird noise.

There are other ways Elvis makes his presence known. The King spent most of his life in the glare of stage lights. At Studio B, lights have been known to dim and even burst without any rational explanation.

It makes the studio workers wonder: Is this the King trying to reach across dimensions to record one more hit?

New Orleans

Elvis was larger than life—in more ways than one.

His presence was a lot like New Orleans: Big. Brassy. Energetic. Not afraid to hide the flamboyant side.

E's spirit matched the Big Easy's spirit. Because portions of Elvis's spirit seemed to remain at places he connected with in real life, it's no surprise that he would leave a hunk of burning love in New Orleans—and maintain that bond even as he left the mortal plane.

That's exactly what happened, according to plenty of stories and legends about Elvis's paranormal preoccupation with the city. When Elvis filmed *Kid Creole*, he lived in the French

Quarter and, by all accounts, he took to the Big Easy and the personalities of its larger-than-life residents like a native.

The stories of Elvis ghost sightings mix with another Big Easy supernatural tradition: the haunted balcony.

The muggy Louisiana heat must draw the spirits that haunt New Orleans outside, because balconies are among the city's most paranormally active spaces. Ethereal images appear on the balconies and then vanish in the blink of an eye. Because New Orleans is one of the most photographed cities, photographic evidence continues to pour in of the haunted-balcony phenomenon.

Tourists who take snapshots of the French Quarter's interesting balconies—and the interesting characters hanging out on those balconies—try to capture this unique architectural feature. But they get a lot more than unusual designs. Sometimes, when they look at the photos, they notice really unusual phenomena, like orbs and shadows. Then there are the shapes that appear in the photos that look very human-like—ones that weren't there when the photographer snapped the picture.

Some say you can see the image of Elvis in many of these spirit pictures. He's just hanging around, like a native. On Royal Street, for instance, not too far from the fantastically haunted LaLaurie Mansion, people have said they've seen—and taken snapshots of—Elvis looking out from a balcony. The ghost of Elvis appears as he did in his Hillbilly Cat younger days. His jet-black hair is slicked black and he wears a white t-shirt.

He looks just like he did in *Kid Creole*, they say.

Whether Elvis's ghost is in Nashville, or at home in Graceland, or hanging out on a balcony in the French Quarter, fans seem happy that their beloved King of Rock and Roll hasn't left the mortal building. It's hard to imagine a world without him.

For fans, Elvis ghost sightings aren't scary. They just prove that the King isn't gone and that the Hillbilly Cat is on the prowl again.

CHAPTER 3

BUDDY HOLLY:

The Night the Music Died (but the Musicians Hung Around)

Rock and roll was barely out of its infancy when the first great tragedy struck the new artform.

It was a mortal blow.

On February 3, 1959, three young men who were changing the shape (and sound) of popular culture climbed into a single-engine Beechcraft Bonanza airplane during a howling Midwestern storm.

While a plane ride in the middle of a brutal Midwestern winter may not have seemed like the brightest idea or the safest choice, the three rock pioneers—Buddy Holly, Ritchie Valens, who was still a teenager at the time, and J. P. Richardson, better known as the Big Bopper—cringed at the alternative. To them, riding the tour bus that was toting an army of musicians who were part of Holly's Winter Dance Party tour was just as chancy—and just as dangerous—as taking a quick plane hop from Clear Lake, Iowa, to their next stop in Moorhead, Minnesota. In fact, earlier in the tour, Carl Bunch, Holly's drummer, almost lost his leg to frostbite because of the bus's faulty heating system. (Valens and Holly, both multi-instrumentalists, filled in as the drummer after the incident.)

Each passenger had other reasons to take the flight. Holly hoped to avoid the rickety old bus and arrive early enough to wash his clothes. Richardson had the flu and wanted some time to recoup.

One mystery, among the dozens of mysteries inspired by the incident, was why Valens wanted to fly. He was the most unlikely air passenger. The rising teen star had a lifelong aversion to flying after witnessing a plane crash in his hometown that claimed the life of one of his classmates.

Holly chartered a plane, but it could only hold three people besides the pilot. After a bit of haggling—and, according to legend, one fateful coin toss—the passengers on the aircraft were selected: Holly, Richardson, and Valens.

That night, the three rock stars and pilot headed into the howling winter night and landed in the haunted legends of rock and roll. The four men were found the next morning among the twisted wreckage of the small plane that was spread out on the fields of an Iowa farm. A lot of people do not realize that there was another victim of the crash. Holly's new bride was pregnant when he decided to embark on the tour to raise money for his growing family. On hearing the news of Holly's death, Maria Elena, his wife, became distraught and miscarried, according to Holly biographers.

Some rock critics said there was yet one more victim—the crash's final victim was rock and roll itself. Holly took the genre to a new level of artistry and creativity. After his death, rock stagnated, turning more toward tame, polished, and marketable acts instead of the raw talents that once made the music so vital. It wouldn't be until the Beatles, true Holly disciples, landed at John F. Kennedy airport about five years later that rock would get its much-needed second wind.

Rock fans and the nation mourned the loss of the talent and sensed the drastic change in the culture. However, residents of the little farming communities near the crash site began to sense that something had changed in the very fabric of the once calm and serene fields.

At first, it was just a feeling. There was something sad about the fields—which was understandable given the immensity of the tragedy. People had an unsettling feeling when they walked around or drove past the site, which soon became an impromptu memorial for the dead rockers. But then people began to report strange incidents near the field that couldn't just be ascribed to emotions or memories.

The most frequently told tale is that a group of Holly fans made a pilgrimage to the crash site on the anniversary of the accident. They wanted to be at that spot on the very day and at the very minute that the crash happened years before.

At the exact time of the anniversary, the group heard noises. They were faint sounds, but the fans believed they heard the clang of twisting metal, like a crash. At first, they speculated that they must have heard a distant car crash, but the roads were abandoned and no reports surfaced of any auto accidents the next day.

Some members of the group said they also heard something else, like screaming, on the night of the anniversary.

This incident could easily be blamed on the overactive imaginations of eager Buddy Holly fans, but there's something that stands in the way of this assessment: other witnesses have reported the same mysterious noises.

Audible phenomena aren't the only indication that the music plays on in Clear Lake. Witnesses have reported "spook lights" near the crash area. Orbs of light flash and roam throughout the acres and acres of farmland. People have observed the activity from the nearby airport. Photographs taken in the area also show odd lights and orbs. For paranormal researchers, this indicates heightened supernatural activity.

Sightings of actual apparitions of Holly and his tour mates are pretty rare at the crash site and memorial at Clear Lake, but they reportedly put on regular shows at other venues. One of those spooky spots is the Rave / Eagles Club in Milwaukee, Wisconsin, which was the site of one of Holly's last shows. Described now as a "super club," the arena was a must-play stop for any band touring the Midwest in those early days of rock and roll.

Besides playing host to some of rock's luminaries, past and present, the hall has a history of paranormal activity. Many musicians have reported seeing someone—someone who looked like Buddy Holly—playing on stage at the Rave / Eagles Club. Others can just sense the spirit of rock's most vital pioneer as they perform.

Holly is just one of the ghosts in the Rave / Eagles Club. He has a captive audience for eternity, according to paranormal researchers. In the club's basement, witnesses have heard children talking and laughing. The creepiest place to witness this phenomenon is at the site of the old swimming pool in the club, once a favorite place for area kids. Concertgoers have passed down a story that the pool was once the scene of a tragic drowning, and many speculate that the sounds of laughter and the occasional scream are just psychic echoes of the event. Paranormal researchers call this a "residual haunting." But since the club was also once used as an athletic club for youth, other people speculate that an unpopular coach is the cause of negative haunting at the building.

The Surf Ballroom, where the fated trio played their last concert, is said to be inhabited by the "presence" of Holly and his musical compatriots. While no one has stepped out and said they've actually seen the ghost of Holly, musicians who have played at the Surf Ballroom have said that they wouldn't be surprised if he did appear. And for seekers of evidence of Holly's after-life legacy, the Surf Ballroom is a premier place to try to contact the singer.

Holly's Hometown Haunts

Holly was no stranger to tours, so it would not be a surprise if his spirit finally wandered back to his hometown of Lubbock, Texas. The City of Lubbock Cemetery, where Holly was laid to rest, is reported to be haunted.

One paranormal research society in Texas has conducted several investigations of the cemetery that indicate there are spirits that haunt it. The hauntings get a lot of play during Halloween in the local media. And according to a local paper, the *Avalanche-Journal*, the cemetery is "very haunted."

If Holly's spirit is still hanging out at the Lubbock Cemetery, he's just one of many, the ghost hunters point out. There are about sixty thousand graves in the massive cemetery. Weird phenomena that have been reported by ghost hunters include orbs and shadow people. The freakiest of all is the story about a "glowing man" who prowls the cemetery like a human torch.

It's hard to say if any of the paranormal activity that's been witnessed at the city cemetery is related to Buddy Holly. But it hasn't stopped fans from coming to his grave and seeking to connect with the spirit of rock and roll's most brilliant pioneer.

Haunted cornfields, city cemeteries, and bars aren't the only places where fans sense Holly's paranormal presence. In an upcoming chapter, we'll discuss how the Texas crooner left a rich, spooky, and perhaps even cursed legacy.

CHAPTER 4

BRIAN JONES:
Like the Ghost of a Rolling Stone

Brian Jones is at the top of the list of tragic, enigmatic figures in rock and roll history. Though he was incredibly talented, his friends said he squandered that talent on booze and drugs. He was intelligent and creative, but spent most of his time with malcontents and hangers-on.

Jones is an enigma that refuses to go away.

A founding member of the Rolling Stones, Jones was born in Cheltenham, England, to two musically gifted parents. He was a natural musician, effortlessly learning how to play guitar and figuring out the intricacies of slide guitar—no easy task. But that's just the beginning. During his career as a Stone, Jones played organ, marimba, recorder, saxophone, dulcimer, accordion, oboe, harpsichord, and autoharp.

He even learned how to play the sitar—a complicated Indian stringed instrument—for songs like "Street Fighting Man" and "Paint It Black."

Jones's prodigious musical abilities were only matched, biographers say, by his drug and alcohol abuse. In a time when drugs were experimental, the multi-instrumentalist was the chief psychedelic laboratory technician for the Rolling Stones. Jones's drug use was one cause for a falling out with the rest of the Rolling Stones. Well, at least, his inability to handle his drugs was one reason for the falling out. Mick Jagger and Keith Richards, who were quickly becoming the band's leaders and principal songwriters, were losing patience with Jones's undependable performances and, sometimes, his antisocial behavior.

I'll just add that when you're kicked out of the Stones for bad behavior, it's really saying something.

Jones himself was disappointed with the band's drift from its blues roots to rock and roll. He considered the commercial rock that Mick and Keith were writing as selling out. A series of arrests and illnesses left the guitarist on even thinner ice. Eventually, Jones was asked to leave the band, although his band mates let him make the decision on how he would like to leave: quit or be fired.

He told the public he had artistic differences with the Stones and that he would venture off on his own. It would be an eternal venture.

The incident on the night of July 2 and the morning of July 3, 1969, is now soaked in mystery and myth, hearsay and conjecture. The body of Brian Jones was discovered in a swimming pool at his estate in East Sussex. The estate was part of the farm once owned by *Winnie-the-Pooh* author A. A. Milne.

The death was ruled an accident. More specifically, the coroner labeled it "death by misadventure." Others aren't so sure. Witnesses have stepped forward to suggest that Jones was murdered, possibly by a few builders who were at the site of the home doing renovation work.

Another conspiracy claimed that there was no accident or homicide: Jones's death was caused by supernatural forces. Jones had grown fearful on the days leading up to his death that he was somehow cursed. The Rolling Stones were no strangers to the world of black magic and the occult. They even named an album *Their Satanic Majesties Request*. Perhaps Jones had felt that these dark forces were now arrayed against him. Friends of Jones said that he was convinced that a shaman had cursed him during a trip to Africa when he was recording a group of African drummers.

One more report indicates that a chilling supernatural prediction was made before the guitar player's demise. The story, told by writer R. Gary Patterson in the book *Take a Walk on the Dark Side*, indicates that shortly before Jones's death, Mick Jagger and girlfriend Marianne Faithfull were tossing I Ching coins, a Chinese fortune-telling system. The I Ching experienced a resurgence in the explorative 1960s rock and roll culture, and Faithfull quickly became a student. Basically, the person seeking guidance tosses a group of coins—usually three coins—and then consults a guide to match the fortune with the pattern of coins.

Two weeks before Jones died, Faithfull tossed the coins and got a combination that meant "death by water." Jagger, a little disconcerted, asked Faithfull to toss the coins again.

She got the same result.

Two weeks later, Jones drowned.

But Faithfull said Jones wasn't really gone. In fact, he visited her. After Jones's death, Faithfull, already under the influence of drugs, fell into a deep depression. Jagger and Faithfull may have felt pangs of guilt because the apparent accident happened so soon after Jones's dismissal from the Rolling Stones and they had ample time to warn him of their dire I Ching prophecy.

Faithfull cut her hair to resemble the hairstyle of Jones. Once, when she looked into the mirror, Faithfull said she actually saw Brian Jones staring at her. Was it his ghost? Or just a hallucination?

Faithfull's drug use and depression resulted in an overdose that brought her to the edge of death. She slipped into a coma and doctors weren't sure that she would survive. In her biography, *Faithfull*, however, she said that while she was in the coma, the spirit of Brian Jones appeared to her. Jones apparently convinced her that she had to return.

Jones's ghost isn't just saving overdose victims. He may still be in the recording business, too.

During an interview with *The Sun*, a UK newspaper, psychic Tony Stockwell was speaking about his show *The Psychic Detective.* The interview, which was recorded for accuracy's sake, was supposed to be just with Tony, but the reporter noticed someone else's voice on the tape. It may have been Jones's.

While the psychic was speaking about an investigation into the death of Jones, the reporter noticed a certain "wail" on the tape during the playback. No one had heard the noise during the interview, and it didn't seem to have any mechanical origin.

The inexplicable sound heard on the tapes came just as Stockwell said, "Brian Jones was the guy who was found dead in his swimming pool. It was believed for years that he was at some sort of drug- or alcohol-fueled party."

The reporter decided to have the tape checked out, and experts agreed that the voice was an EVP—an electronic voice phenomenon. An expert who worked on *White Noise*, a movie about the dead contacting the living through EVPs, concluded that the tapes and the noise heard on the tapes were legitimate.

Some of Jones's friends and associates do not have trouble believing that the spirit of the guitarist lingers and is eager to communicate. Jones was familiar with the occult. Kenneth Anger, a movie producer and Stones hanger-on, believed that Jones and the band were involved in witchcraft. He said that Jones, Keith Richards, and Anita Pallenberg, who was girlfriend to both Richards and Jones, had formed a little coven in the band.

"The occult unit within the Stones was Keith and Anita and Brian," Anger said. "You see, Brian was a witch too."

Could the weird noise on the interview be an attempt by Jones to communicate his displeasure that the reason for his death was incorrect? Was he trying to alert the reporter about the murder? Or had the ghost of Jones become attached to the psychic? After all, lots of psychics talk about spirits following them home from their haunted environs.

No one knows the answers to these questions for sure. But it does seem that if the spirit of Jones is reaching out to reinvestigate the incident, that message may have finally gotten through.

In 2009, police reopened Jones's case to investigate those charges, according to *Rolling Stone* magazine. Recent reports suggest not an accident, but foul play. A deathbed confession of one of the partygoers has made it through the entertainment rumor mill. Several people who were close to Brian and were at the party have said they were threatened to not talk about Jones's "accident."

The real question is, will this investigation finally allow the restless spirit of one of the Rolling Stones' most restless members to rest in peace?

CHAPTER 5

JOHN LENNON:

A Magical Mystery Tour of the Fab Four's Paranormal Legacy

There is no place on earth where music and magic mix more effortlessly than in the nations that make up the British Isles. Faerie music and spirit songs travel on the breezes across the fields and bogs, lakes and streams, and the cities and towns of England, Wales, Scotland, Ireland, and Northern Ireland.

Is it any wonder, then, that one of the world's greatest bands is English? And is it any wonder that ghost stories and tales of mysticism followed these lads from Liverpool?

While John Lennon, George Harrison, Paul McCartney, and Ringo Starr were born in the land that produced great magicians, like Merlin, and fairies and pixies, there was nothing magical about the Beatles' humble beginnings. The group rose from obscurity in the rough, working-class port city of Liverpool, which is about as far from Camelot as you can imagine.

But through hard work and unbridled talent, the Beatles rose to dominate the pop music charts.

While they did, they revolutionized music, too. Before the Beatles, with only a few exceptions, bands played, engineers recorded, and songwriters wrote. After the Beatles, musicians became self-supportive entertainment machines capable of writing, recording, and performing their own material.

The Beatles also popularized the concept album—a collection of songs that represented a theme, like *Sgt. Pepper's Lonely Hearts Club Band*.

Their recording techniques, often created with the help of their master producer, George Martin, set the bar for future pop music works of art. In fact, it wasn't really until the Beatles that pop music was respected as an artform at all.

There's a saying that those who are blessed are equally cursed. Though the Beatles were blessed with talent and timing, it's hard to dismiss the dark and haunted cloud that hung over the band.

One of the founding members of the band was Stuart Sutcliffe. His friend John Lennon begged him to be in his new band. After all, the band needed a bass player—and Stu's James Dean–like looks didn't hurt either.

But Stu was more of a painter and less of a bassist. His paintings—modern avant-garde pieces—frequently won awards at Liverpool art shows. But Stu, a dutiful friend, wanted to help, and the Beatles did need a bass player, even if he wasn't exactly the most solid four-string player around.

Stu accompanied the Beatles on their sluggish rise to fame, smashing out rock and roll in sweaty, beer-fueled sessions in Liverpool clubs and then into the beer halls of Germany.

It was shortly after the Beatles played its now legendary sets in Hamburg, Germany, that Stu decided to stay behind with his new German girlfriend to explore his career as a painter.

The Beatles never saw Stu again.

On April 10, 1962, just a few months before Beatlemania gripped Europe, Stu died of what most experts speculate was a cerebral hemorrhage. For years he had suffered from intense headaches and the occasional sensitivity to lights—all symptoms of a hemorrhage.

But John Lennon felt that being a Beatle killed Stu. Once, the band was jumped by a bunch of toughs, called Teddy Boys, after a show. Stu, who was smaller than the rest of his band mates, took a particular thrashing. He was kicked repeatedly in the head. The death may also have been tough on Lennon because his mother had been killed, hit by a car, when he was young.

Stu's death and his spirit, people said, continued to haunt the Beatles. Yoko Ono, Lennon's wife, said there wasn't a day that went by that Lennon didn't talk about Stu.

Stu was just one of the sad spirits to drift in—and then out—of the lives of the Beatles. Brian Epstein, their manager and one of the men credited with discovering the band, died in 1967. His spirit, too, cast a long shadow over the band. Fans say that without Epstein's guiding spirit, the band spiraled out of control, finally breaking up in 1970.

The band even planned to contact Epstein through a seance shortly after his death. Lennon was one of the instigators of the seance, which is surprising. Despite his interest in metaphysics and the occult, Lennon was the band's cynic. Still, he was convinced that there was life after death. He once said he was an optimist about eternity, adding in a 1969 interview with David Wigg, "I'd like to live to a ripe old age, with Yoko only, you know. And I'm not afraid of dying." There's no word whether the band did eventually contact Brian, or even if they went through with the seance. The band and their circle of friends were secretive.

Cilla Black, a friend of Epstein and the Beatles, begged out of the seance, according to Bill Harry, who wrote about the incident in the Beatles Browser. Black was afraid they actually would contact Lennon. "They wanted me to sit in with them, but I didn't," she said. "I mean, if he had shown up, I wouldn't have known what to say and anyway, it would only have made his death worse."

John's Ghost

Haunted by the deaths of close friends and family members throughout his life, Lennon was convinced that life did continue after death.

"I'm not afraid of death because I don't believe in it," Lennon said in the 1969 interview with David Wigg. "It's just getting out of one car and into another."

Later, Lennon himself proved that life wasn't a temporary assignment. Band members, friends, and family reported they had otherworldly run-ins with the Beatle after his tragic death. Lennon was shot on December 8, 1980, by Mark David Chapman, whom most described as an obsessed Beatles fan.

After Lennon's death, the reports of strange encounters with the former rock star began to trickle in. One of the more amazing incidents occurred when his son was filming a movie about whales. About eighteen years after Lennon's murder,

Julian Lennon, who showed he had his old man's gift for making music when he produced a string of hits in the 1980s, was taking part in an Aboriginal ceremony while on location in Australia, according to the *Daily Express*, a British newspaper. During the ceremony, a tribal elder passed a white feather to Julian.

The leader of the tribe had no way of knowing it, but the feather had secret significance to Julian. John had told his son that if anything happened to him, Julian should look for a white feather and know that he was there, looking out for his son. Julian never told anyone about the conversation.

John delivered another fine-feathered-friend message, this time to his band mates. The breakup of the Beatles was not a pleasant affair for the formerly close-knit band. They had spent their hardscrabble childhoods dreaming of stardom together, spent more than a decade together struggling to become rock stars, and then spent another decade together dealing with the stress of being rock stars. When the group decided to go their separate ways, each member felt wounded on some level.

When Lennon was murdered, the surviving Beatles were wracked with grief. It was more than just their friend's death that saddened them. Deep inside, the rest of the band knew that a complete reconciliation would never be achieved. The remaining Beatles did try to gain some closure by recording together one last time. After finding an unreleased Lennon track called "Free as a Bird," the band met to add their own touches to the song in the mid-1990s as part of the *Beatles Anthology* project.

During a picture-taking session at a farm, the three Beatles were stunned when a huge white peacock walked into the shot at the last second. They immediately took the bird as a sign that John was present.

"That's John. Spooky, eh? It was like John was hanging around. We felt that all through the recording," McCartney said, according to an article in Unexplained Mysteries, among other sources.

Another incident that occurred during the recording sessions solidified the belief that John was somehow watching over them. After recording a song late at night, the band members listened back to the track. They were stunned when, as the song ended, a garbled static erupted. The band swore they heard the name "John Lennon" in the distortion.

"We were like, 'It's John. He likes it!'" McCartney said.

It could have been a case of electronic voice phenomena (EVP). Paranormal investigators believe that the voices of spirits, which are often inaudible, can be captured using sensitive recording devices.

Was Lennon using this EVP as a way to get a little studio time with his old band mates and join the lads one more time?

According to ghost hunters in Liverpool, Lennon is still hanging out in his old hometown. Most of the accounts come from the area around Menlove Avenue in the city, the neighborhood where Lennon grew up. In one story, a man walking his dog approached the gates of Strawberry Fields, the one-time orphanage that Lennon and McCartney made famous in the song by the same name. The dog—uncharacteristically—dug in his paws and refused to take another step. The man was flabbergasted. Then he looked up and saw a man with long hair and spectacles near the gates. The man looked exactly like Lennon. Standing next to Lennon's ghost appeared to be an older woman, perhaps Lennon's Aunt Mimi, who raised him.

The man picked up his pooch and practically ran home.

When he arrived safely back at his house, the man told his wife that he had just seen the ghost of John Lennon. He described the two ghosts to his wife, who was not really a Beatles fan. The man's wife then claimed she had seen the same apparitions on a few occasions. As someone who wasn't really familiar with the band, she had never made the John Lennon–Aunt Mimi connection.

Celebrity Sighting

John doesn't just manifest for his old band mates and the occasional unsuspecting dog walker. He's been known to pop in on fellow celebrities.

In 1989, actress Robin Givens moved into a West Hollywood home once owned by John Lennon shortly after her break-up with boxer Mike Tyson. The Tyson-Givens stormy relationship was fodder for every scandal sheet and tabloid in its day.

Givens's life was in a near constant state of disarray, and moving into Lennon's old place was the first step of her new life. She told the *Boston Herald* that she immediately sensed Lennon's spirit in the place. It was more of a presence, she said. But she had no real, tangible evidence that Lennon was still in the building—until he decided to sing to her.

One day, as Givens went about her daily routine, she heard what sounded like singing. She stopped and listened closely. Now, she not only heard singing, but she also could tell it was the voice of a man. Givens looked for the source, but never saw the body. As she listened more intently, she realized it was John Lennon.

The ghostly singing didn't frighten her. In fact, in those tough times, it may have offered her consolation that another celebrity who had had run-ins with the press as well was on her side.

The Dakota

It wouldn't take much to convince people that the apartment building in New York City called "the Dakota" is haunted. Roman Polanski didn't need to be convinced. The film director used the mystical-looking New York City landmark located on Seventy-second Street and Central Park West as the setting for his classic horror film *Rosemary's Baby*.

Frankenstein's monster even lived in the Dakota. Well, Boris Karloff, who brought the monster to life in several movies, was a resident.

The Dakota just plain looks haunted. Some say the building's spires, besides offering impressive views of the cityscape, give it a supernatural, otherworldly look. Other people—including a long list of former and current residents—say that the building's haunted reputation is well deserved. The building is packed with tales of ghosts who walk its halls and of otherworldly encounters.

On December 8, 1980, the building actually lived up to its horror-movie reputation. Just steps away from the safety of his apartment, Lennon was shot and killed by Mark David Chapman. The death set off a spontaneous wave of memorials for the departed rock star. Thousands of fans poured into the streets around the Dakota. The spirit of Lennon was tangible in the crowd, according to journalists who reported on the event.

The crowds of people eventually left the impromptu memorial in front of the Dakota. Lennon stayed. His spirit is now one more of the building's many ghostly tenants.

One musician who lived near the Dakota reported that he saw a figure that looked exactly like Lennon standing in the entrance to the building. Maybe it was a look-alike, but the musician also said the figure had a mysterious light that surrounded him. A good pair of round glasses, an "I Love New York" shirt, and a long-haired wig may help you create a decent Lennon disguise, but surrounding yourself with an ethereal aura is much more difficult to pull off, the witness declared.

Besides the ghost of John Lennon, whom many have claimed to see walking the halls of the Dakota and crossing the sidewalk, as he did on that fateful December evening, the apartment building reportedly has a few other spirits to keep him company in the afterlife.

A group of construction workers back in the 1960s said they saw the ghosts of children dressed in clothing from a different era in the Dakota, according to an About.com article. The same article indicated that a group of painters also saw the ghost of a girl in similar old-fashioned clothing a few years after the construction workers had their paranormal run-in. The kids were probably the same age as many children who became entranced by the Beatles' infectious melodies and driving beats in the 1960s. It's interesting to speculate, though, that maybe it's not just a Beatle who lives on. Maybe Beatlemania survives in the afterlife as well?

CHAPTER 6

LED ZEPPELIN:

Stairway to Heaven—or the Alternative

There are some bands that are naturally haunted.

There are some rock bands that have had hauntings thrust upon them.

And then there is Led Zeppelin.

They worked hard to be haunted.

Few bands have embraced the occult and the dark arts as much as Led Zeppelin, the band that became the model of what would eventually become known as a superband during the hard-living, harder-rocking 1970s. Like a mystic fog drifting across the shire, Led Zeppelin arose from the ashes of the Yardbirds, a group that spawned the careers of noted guitar slingers Jeff Beck and Eric Clapton.

The new band originally went by the name the New Yardbirds until the Who's madcap drummer, Keith Moon, suggested another name. Moon was dismissive of Jimmy Page's new project and said that the New Yardbirds would go over like a lead balloon with fans. And the new moniker was born. Propelled by the guitar mastery of Jimmy Page, the ethereal vocals of Robert Plant, the explosive drumming of John Bonham, and the extraordinary bass guitar playing of John Paul Jones, the quartet is considered a rock and roll dream team. Led Zeppelin's members were all recognized for their mastery of their musical instruments.

They may have been the dream team of rock and roll, but there were hints of nightmares stalking the band.

These allegations indicated that another type of power fueled this outrageous band of prodigies—and this force is the reason Led Zep is considered one of rock's most unabashedly haunted bands. Pop culture writers and rock historians say that Led Zeppelin came under the exclusive management services not of a human impresario, but of occult forces. Jimmy Page makes no excuses. He has always been interested in magic, and not just the pull-a-rabbit-out-of-a-hat type of magic.

Page became captivated by England's premier dark magician, Aleister Crowley, also referred to as the wickedest man in the world. The man who would one day go by the numerical nickname of "666" was born on October 12, 1875. On paper, little Aleister had a lot going for him. He was born to the upper crust of English society. His father was an engineer, but grew so wealthy from his shares in a family brewing business that he was able to retire early. His mother was born into an aristocratic family. Both parents were deeply religious Christians who read the Bible every morning at breakfast to their boy. They certainly wasted their breath.

Crowley showed his diabolical nature at a young age, arguing with his religious instructors at an Evangelical Christian school his parents forced him to attend. But he wasn't just making theological arguments; Crowley was testing the limits of Britain's strict moral codes as he experimented with sex and paid visits to the homes of female prostitutes.

His father's money provided him with the best college education, but even at Trinity College, Crowley's desire to be the big devil on campus was insatiable. He spent most of his time mountaineering and writing erotic poetry. When he wasn't climbing mountains or searching the thesaurus for a word that rhymes with "luck," Crowley delved into the occult and esoterica. His philosophy—always somewhat extreme—took an even harder turn toward the evil side as he began to experiment with the "dark arts."

Over the years, as Crowley vagabonded from one country to the next, from one adventure to another, his reputation as a magician—and a degenerate—grew legendary. All sorts of bizarre activity were ascribed to Crowley and his growing band of followers, including orgies, Satanic rituals, and even crimes.

We know a lot of rock stars who became famous for being infamous. Alice Cooper, Ozzy Osbourne, Marilyn Manson … need I go on? Well, Crowley paved the way for the famously infamous. Always well stocked with the latest drugs, he was quite the hit at celebrity parties. My favorite Crowley story is about the time he reportedly met novelist Theodore Dreiser at a party and handed the writer some peyote. Dreiser started to feel the effects of the psychedelic and asked for a doctor.

According to a post by rock historian Peter Watts, Crowley reportedly told him he didn't know about a doctor, "but there's a first-class undertaker on the corner of 33rd and 6th."

Never one to worry about bad publicity, Crowley wrote extensively about his experiments with both the devil and debauchery. After his death, this literary legacy would serve as a guide for budding occultists, seekers of magick, and even a few rock stars—like Page. The guitarist, rock historians say, immersed himself in magick and Crowley lore. He even bought an occult bookshop, a move he said was a necessity since he couldn't find the right titles or enough books to satisfy his ravenous appetite for the supernatural. Page's fascination with the occult didn't stop with reading Crowley biographies and magical textbooks. With royalties pouring in from some of the highest-selling albums of the 1970s, like *Led Zeppelin IV* and *Physical Graffiti*, Page had plenty of money to spend on his hobby, or, as he may call it, his mission.

One of the first purchases Page made with this windfall was an estate in Scotland once owned by Crowley. There wasn't much interest in the place, called Boleskine House, from buyers. The home was reportedly haunted and had a dark reputation among the villagers who lived near the estate, on the eastern shore of the uber-mystical Loch Ness—yep, the same Loch Ness with the sea monster.

Crowley had reportedly bought the mansion because it fit perfectly with a spell he was trying to perform. The spell required an isolated home with doors positioned in a certain direction to make the intonation of the spell effective.

According to a legend that pre-dated even Crowley's ownership of the estate, a church had been built on the site. The church, with its congregation trapped inside, burned to the ground one day. In another story about the residence, a caretaker of the estate went insane and tried to kill his wife. The place was like *The Shining* and *Poltergeist* all wrapped into one real estate package.

Far from scaring off the Antichrist, the tales of malevolent spirits and horrific deaths made the estate an easy sale for some lucky realtor. Crowley, who was embarking on his most important magical work, wrote that he was becoming more and more attracted to the home because of its mystical properties.

Crowley said Boleskine was darker, literally and figuratively, than any home he had ever lived in—probably another selling point. He said that during some magical rites, he had to use artificial light to see his spellbooks even though it was mid-afternoon. There were also reports of "shadow people," filmy shadows that flitted around the halls and rooms of Boleskine.

The darkness seemed to deepen when Crowley dove into his magical work.

One day, as legend has it, a butcher showed up at Boleskine to pick up Crowley's order. Crowley was upset that the butcher continued to ring the doorbell while he was meditating. Grabbing a piece of paper, Crowley scribbled down his order for the butcher. What Crowley didn't know was that the piece of paper he grabbed for his meat order actually had a spell written on the other side. When the butcher got back to the shop, he started to fill Crowley's order. The butcher, who was an expert at carving and slicing meat, cut off all the fingers of his right hand with a single errant swing of a cleaver. The people who heard about the butcher's visit to Boleskine knew immediately whom to blame for the mishap.

Crowley's spell was so powerful, the villagers said, that it had accidentally cursed the poor meat cutter.

Crowley compounded the effects of the paranormal activity by admitting that he summoned demons while he performed his magical work. In one instance, Crowley said a demon, summoned from the desert, took possession of his body, transforming the chunky, middle-aged man into a young, beautiful woman. Crowley's followers said they were protected from the demon by a magic circle. However, when one of the followers looked down to write something the demon had said, the creature leaped into the circle and attacked the horrified participants.

The supernatural forces did not diminish when Crowley left the home. Page and his friends reported strange sightings and events as residents of Boleskine. Kenneth Anger, a friend of Page, reported that he witnessed strange events at Boleskine. A large painting levitated off the wall and settled onto the ground while a group of witnesses, including Anger, watched in horror.

That was nothing.

Page's caretaker said he awoke one night and heard something at his bedroom door. He said it sounded like a large—and angry—dog growling at the closed door. The sound of claws scratching across the floor kept the caretaker up all night. He waited until daylight to investigate.

Page told a *Rolling Stone* reporter that many of his friends had witnessed strange activity while staying with him at the haunted estate.

"A man was beheaded there [at Boleskine], and sometimes you can hear a head rolling down. I haven't actually heard it, but a friend of mine, who is extremely straight and doesn't know anything about anything like that at all, heard it. He thought it was the cats bungling about. I wasn't there at the time, but, he told the help, 'Why don't you let the cats out at night? They make a terrible racket, rolling about in the halls.'"

But the cats were locked in a room at night. Then, the staff members told Page's now frightened friend that what he had heard had a far more diabolical and paranormal source.

Page added a cryptic statement during the *Rolling Stone* interview. Since Page said he had never heard the head roll, the reporter guessed that the guitarist had never had interaction with spirits in the home.

"I didn't say that," Page bristled. "I just said I didn't hear the head roll."

The implication is that Page had indeed witnessed supernatural activity, but his interaction with the spirit world went way beyond a few bumps in the night.

Whether the paranormal events got to be too much for Page or the bill for the mansion's upkeep was too high, reports are that the guitarist sold his beloved Boleskine in the early 1990s.

However, Page's interest in the world of spirits—both good and evil—followed him beyond Boleskine and throughout his career. The band, most likely under Page's direction, made little attempt to hide this occult connection. In some pressings of *Led Zeppelin III*, the words "Do what thou wilt" are etched into the album itself. The phrase is Crowley's most well-known reference to his magical philosophy.

Another phrase that crops up in Page's magical lexicon, "So mote be it," is written on other versions of *Led Zeppelin*

III. The phrase is used by magicians, Wiccans, and Witchcraft practitioners and serves as an incantation that signifies the end of a spell. For people who are schooled in magick and the occult, this is code for "Amen."

Besides the cryptic signs and codes on album covers, Page said that the music the band produced itself resulted from a magical process.

"I'll leave this subject by saying the four musical elements of Led Zeppelin making a fifth is magick into itself," Page said. "That's the alchemical process."

In a later chapter, we'll discuss another part of Led Zeppelin's haunted legacy—the Led Zep curse.

CHAPTER 7

JIM MORRISON:
The Once and Future Lizard King

Some rock stars have seen ghosts. Some rock stars have become ghosts. Leave it to Jim Morrison to be the only rock star who said he was a ghost.

The first ghost story to attach itself to the Doors, one of most experimental rock bands of the 1960s, actually occurred years before the Los Angeles–based band was even formed. But the following tale has become central to the mythological and shamanistic vibe of the Doors, a band that made the paranormal totally normal.

The Doors' Dionysian lead singer, Morrison, told his band mates and friends that as a Navy brat, his family moved often. During one trip across the American Southwest, the family came upon the scene of a horrible accident. The way Morrison told the story, he saw the bodies of several Native Americans strewn across the roadside. He said that as the traumatized family passed the wreck, he felt the spirits of the victims enter his body.

"The reaction I get now thinking about it, looking back, is that the souls of the ghosts of those dead Indians ... maybe one or two of 'em ... were just running around freaking out, and just leaped into my soul," Morrison said in his spoken-word piece *An American Prayer*. "And they're still there."

His art and his tumultuous life—which tragically ended when he drowned in the bathroom of an apartment in Paris at the age of twenty-seven—was seen by many critics and fans as a journey to exorcise those spirits, or maybe those spirits turned Morrison into a shaman to exorcise the spirits of his fans.

Even the origin of the band's name is emblematic of the quest to find, in Morrison's words, "the other side." The band mates picked the name from a line in William Blake's poem "The Marriage of Heaven and Hell": "If the doors of perception were cleansed every thing would appear to man as it is, infinite."

By all accounts, Morrison embraced shamanism and the occult as a way to reach the other side, the transcendent realm of reality. Morrison believed that true art and true poetry resided there. Paranormal researchers say true ghosts reside there, too.

Those occult connections followed Morrison as he blazed through stardom. Biographers suggest he was married in a Celtic Pagan ceremony in June of 1970. The woman he reportedly married, Patricia Kennealy-Morrison, was a high priestess of the Celtic Pagan tradition.

It's no surprise to occult experts that Morrison's spirit still crosses the divide between life and death on a regular basis. Witnesses have seen his spirit in the unlikeliest spots. Of course, for Morrison, there's no such thing as an unlikely spot for a haunting.

Our first story of a Morrison ghost sighting seems to show that the singer—who throughout his life tried to distance himself from his family (his father was a U.S. Navy admiral)—might still be a bit nostalgic about his old childhood haunts. As a youth and teenager, Morrison lived in Arlington, Virginia, a prosperous suburb of Washington DC that served as a bedroom community for government workers and military officers like his father.

People who knew the young Jim Morrison said he didn't stand out. He was a little overweight and his hair was a bit too long. He didn't leave much of an impression. But, according to the woman who lived in his former house, he left a spiritual impression.

Rhonda Baron, who lived in the home, told a Washington, DC area television news channel that Morrison still haunts the residence. She's seen him—and even felt him. Baron said that the spirit of Jim Morrison lay down beside her when she was in bed. She said the spirit looked like Morrison but had a "hazy" aura around the body. Morrison's spirit was transparent, so Baron could look completely through the form. As she lay there, stunned, she felt the bed sink in, and then the spirit turned and looked at her. Baron said it was one of three encounters she had in the old bedroom of "little Jimmy," as Morrison was known around the neighborhood.

Morrison seems just as restless now as he did wandering the country and the world as a rock poet in the late 1960s. He appears to have an affinity for bathrooms, too, according to our next story.

Morrison's Bathroom

If I made a list of places that Jim Morrison would most likely haunt, a Mexican restaurant wouldn't be at the top. I don't know if it would even make it on the list. Just about every bar and dive in Los Angeles County, sure. But a Mexican restaurant? There's no evidence in my research that he had a special love of Mexican cuisine.

But workers, patrons, and owners of a little restaurant in West Hollywood called Mexico say the spirit of Jim Morrison pays regular—how should I say—visits to the bathroom there. The restaurant is located on Santa Monica Boulevard, a regular haunt for the Doors back in the day. The general manager of the restaurant claims that Morrison's spirit can be felt all over the establishment, but—and there's no way to put this delicately—most of the encounters happen in the bathroom. Why the bathroom, you ask? Did the burrito not agree with the Lizard King?

Well, actually, the restaurant used to be part of the Doors' recording studio, office, and general party spot. Morrison recorded the vocals of the band's iconic "L.A. Woman" in the very stall that is now the restaurant's lavatory.

Christine Chilcote, an office manager for the restaurant, attributes the range of paranormal phenomena experienced at the eatery to Morrison. Lights pop off at strange times, and the bathroom door jiggles all by itself, something that Chilcote says is "inexplicable."

Larry Nicola, the restaurant's owner, told AOL News that the strange noises that emanate from within the building unnerved him so much that he called in spiritual help.

"The building moans and breathes and makes sounds I can't explain. We had someone come in before we opened up, to do a 'spiritual cleaning' to try and put everything at peace, but in the end they told us, 'Sorry, whatever is here is not leaving.'"

Morrison may not be leaving the restaurant any time soon, but according to our next report, he does pop over to a bar for a little fun on occasion.

The Lizard King Visits the Viper Room

The Viper Room, once one of Los Angeles's hottest clubs, has been the scene of both pure joy and horrible tragedy—usually on the same night.

The nightclub was thrust into the headlines when actor River Phoenix died of an overdose on Halloween outside the club. No one is sure if River's ghost haunts the club, but there are plenty of reports that there's something paranormal going on in the Viper Room.

According to singer-songwriter-poet Otep Shamaya, something haunts the Viper Room, and the spirit may be Jim Morrison, or the ghost of some Doors fan. She told an interviewer for BlogsnRoses.com that she and her band mates were preparing for a show in the club and were running through the pre-performance ritual of sound tests and light checks.

While the band was onstage, a light—suddenly and inexplicably—turned on. There was no doubt about it: the light was focused directly on the musicians on stage.

Otep asked the crew to turn off the light. The crew would have been happy to oblige ... except they said they never turned on the light. They told the band members that the club was haunted and added that the ghost was responsible for the lighting malfunction. The band laughed off the suggestion.

But then the sound engineer joined the debate on the paranormal. He, too, insisted there were spirits in the bar. As he recounted stories about the ghosts to the band, the Doors' song "Roadhouse Blues" began to blast through the speakers. No one was near the sound equipment. One verse of the song pounded through the speakers and then, just as abruptly as the song started, it quit.

Otep told the interviewer: "The sound guy goes, 'Oh, then you know Jim Morrison. That's his ghost. He haunts us here.' I just got a little bit of a chill talking about it."

Come On, Baby, Take My Picture

Brett Meisner is a rock historian and a fan of the Doors, so it wasn't unusual for him to visit the famous grave of Jim Morrison in Paris. But what happened at that graveyard on his trip in 1997 was unusual, even for a devoted Doors fan.

Meisner reportedly captured photographic evidence that Morrison's spirit continues to make his presence known. It's a presence that Meisner says he continues to feel—and it's not always a good thing to have around. During his pilgrimage to Morrison's grave in the city's famous Père Lachaise Cemetery, Meisner stopped to pose in front of Morrison's graffiti-pocked headstone as his assistant took the picture. On first glance, the fan didn't notice anything paranormal about the picture. There was a cloudy image in it, but Meisner said the imperfection never prompted deeper inspection. He pretty much ignored it.

According to Meisner, a series of strange events occurred after his visit to the grave—events that caused him to think he had experienced some type of supernatural encounter. His marriage dissolved. A friend of his died of an overdose—an incident that Meisner said had an eerie similarity to Morrison's own demise.

The string of misfortunes made Meisner think that darker forces were at work. But what did he do wrong? How did he come in contact with this force? Eventually, he decided to take another look at the picture. That's when he saw, in the cloudy haze of the photo, an unmistakable image of the Doors' lead singer.

Meisner has since had his photo analyzed by experts. Some were impressed enough to include it in a book on spirit photography called *Ghosts Caught on Film 2: Photographs of the Unexplained.*

Morrison was preceded in death by another 1960s rock icon—Janis Joplin. She, too, left her mark on pop music history. She also left a restless spirit. We'll track down some of those ghost stories next.

CHAPTER 8

JANIS JOPLIN:
Take Another Piece of My Haunt

Janis Joplin was a lonely girl from Port Arthur, Texas, who rode her soulful voice and creative genius out of a series of small-town miseries and into rock and roll stardom in one of the most stunning examples of artistic invention and reinvention.

Along the way, though, she left more than pieces of her heart as she traveled gypsy-like from city to city, hotel room to hotel room, and auditorium to auditorium; she left a piece of her soul in spots, too.

In 1970, Joplin died of a heroin overdose in a hotel room. She was twenty-seven—another member of the cursed 27 Club. Years before, Joplin had somewhat revealed her self-fulfilling prophecy when she said, "People, whether they know it or not, like their blues singers miserable. They like their blues singers to die afterwards."

She was one of the "big three" rock stars who died due to overindulgence in the early 1970s. Jimi Hendrix and Jim

Morrison broke on through to the other side, too. Many paranormal experts suggest that when young people die suddenly, they often do not make the transition to the other side peacefully. These souls want to remain in this world, or perhaps they just can't process what happened. Sometimes young souls who pass on think they are too young to die. Joplin, who was described by most who knew her as a tenacious but carefree spirit, may fit that description.

She was full of energy. She loved life. And she wasn't ready to surrender just yet.

Hotel Room Haunt

The stories about Janis Joplin's ghost began almost immediately after her death, according to folklorists and ghost hunters in Los Angeles. Joplin passed away in Room 105 of the Landmark Hotel—now called the Highland Gardens Hotel. Located close to the Sunset Strip, which was a musical mecca in the late 1960s, the hotel became a convenient place for rock stars and celebrities to stay—and a great place to party.

The Sunset Strip was party central in the 1960s. Spirits were high, the music was loud, and drugs flowed easily from the Strip. That's why Joplin stationed herself at the hotel: so she was near the music and near the action. It all ended for Joplin in that hotel, and now, the room where she stayed and where they found her lifeless body has gone from party hotspot to paranormal hotspot.

Numerous guests who have stayed in Room 105 have reported a mix of strange happenings and paranormal outbreaks during their visits, ranging from the merely odd to the wildly outrageous. Since no one has ever reported seeing an apparition, it's hard to tell who—or what—is really behind the activity, but the blame seems to fall on poor Joplin—something she's probably used to.

When witnesses describe the paranormal activity in the room, it does sound like Janis's M.O., though. Joplin, or Pearl, as her friends called her, had a mischievous side, and the activity has a practical-joke quality to it. People have complained that the phones ring and when they answer, there's no one on the other line. Lights turn on and off by themselves, too.

The temperature of the room also varies wildly. Sometimes it's too cold, sometimes it's too hot. The thermostat doesn't seem to help. To paranormal researchers, temperature fluctuations can indicate the presence of supernatural forces. When a spirit enters the physical plane, the energy is pulled from the space and the temperature drops, according to paranormal experts. When the spirit exits, the temperature quickly returns to normal, causing a spike in heat. Friends described Janis as a force of nature, so it's no surprise to them that she could be a force of supernature who messes with the temperature settings in a room.

There are also reports that synchronistic events have occurred that are tied to the singer's life and career. One guest wrote in a review of her stay in the room that the visit had been filled with hints that Joplin still haunted it. The guest had downloaded a computer app that, according to the app developer, can detect the presence of ghosts or spiritual entities by flashing random words. The guest said the word "Texas" flashed on the screen of her phone, as well as the word "Mama."

Neither the guest nor her husband figured out the connection, but a quick check of Janis's bio on the Internet allowed all the pieces of the puzzle to fall in place. Janis was from Texas and had an intense love-hate (but mostly hate) relationship with the state. Of course, she was partial to the word "Mama," too, using it in lyrics and song titles. She even had an album named *I Got Dem Ol' Kozmic Blues Again Mama!*

This couple's excursion into haunted rock and roll jibes with a lot of other encounters in Room 105. But the paranormal energy apparently isn't confined to the room. Pictures in the lobby fall off the wall and doors slam—without any apparent cause. The phones also ring erratically—with no caller on the other end of the line.

The debate continues about whether this means Joplin is actually haunting the hotel at all. Others say that it would be just like Janis to wander the halls, looking for a little mischief.

Studio Haunts

Joplin didn't leave just one haunted spot; she left a trail of haunts. Most of her friends and colleagues aren't surprised. Joplin had a roaming spirit in life—and in death.

Sunset Sound Studio 1, where Joplin spent the last remaining hours of her life, is reportedly one of the spots in L.A. where the singer's spirit likes to hang out with kindred musical spirits.

One rock group, Transmatic, was recording in the studio—and was hoping a little of the musical magic that shaped Joplin's career would rub off on their own musical ambitions.

And it did—but in ways the band really wasn't expecting.

Transmatic's lead singer told a newspaper reporter that during the recording session, "weird occurrences" happened. The band had laid down some tracks digitally, and they sounded fine. But later, when the band listened to the tracks again, the instruments were out of tune. Neither the band nor the engineers who were most familiar with the equipment had an explanation for the phenomena.

The band painstakingly rerecorded the tracks.

Since Jim Morrison's ghost is one spirit suspect who haunts the studio, some theorists blame the Doors' lead singer for the out-of-tune instruments. But others see Pearl's handprints all over the haunted activity. Joplin—who was a bit of a purist—may have been messing with the band for going digital and using all that fancy electronic equipment.

CHAPTER 9

"MAMA" CASS ELLIOT:

Of Mamas, Papas, and the Paranormal

The people who knew Cass Elliot said that everything about her was larger than life. She had a big personality, a big voice, and a big heart. Her spirit was just as gigantic and just as relentless. When she died of a heart attack in 1974, those same people had no trouble believing that this relentless, larger-than-life spirit would not meekly pass over from the narrow confines of our everyday mortal world.

When stories began to appear that the ghost of Elliot—one of the key members of the Mamas and the Papas—was appearing at various sites throughout the world, her friends probably thought, "I told you so."

Elliot died in 1974 in a flat in London owned by singer Harry Nilsson—the same place where the Who's drummer, Keith Moon, would later die. But we'll save that for another chapter.

Like so many other events in Elliot's life, her death seemed especially tragic. She had great timing—and terrible timing. The singer passed away just as her solo career started to take off and just as she began to leave the dark career shadow that followed her after the breakup of the Mamas and the Papas. There is no truth, by the way, to the claims that she died eating a sandwich. She was tired after the final show in a series of standing-room-only concerts at the London Palladium. Elliot went to sleep and suffered a heart attack. A half-eaten sandwich was found in the room—which fueled the rumors. But there was no evidence that she choked on the food, according to the medical examiners who investigated the case. The rumor lingered for decades as a cheap swipe at Mama Cass's weight problem by comedians who couldn't find better, more original material.

It's not shocking that the ghost of Elliot is appearing so much as it is to whom she is appearing. The folks who have had an afterworld encounter with Elliot aren't the random crazy fans; they are some of the biggest stars, and they were all willing to go public with their stories of encounters with Elliot's ghost.

Comedian and actor Dan Aykroyd said he had a run-in with a ghost in his home—a mansion where Cass had lived. Over the years that he and his wife, actress Donna Dixon, stayed in the house on Woodrow Wilson Drive in Los Angeles, the couple had a string of unexplained events happen that convinced them that the home—a sprawling house with five bedrooms and five and a half baths tucked in its nearly five-thousand-square-foot interior—was haunted.

So, you're probably thinking that the star of *Saturday Night Live* and *Driving Miss Daisy* was just being funny or maybe drumming up interest to revive the *Ghostbusters* franchise. Maybe. But maybe not.

After all, Aykroyd has spoken of his great respect for the field of paranormal research and sports an impressive paranormal research pedigree himself. His great-grandfather was a leader in the Spiritualist movement, and his family, according to Aykroyd, was "steeped" in Spiritualism, mediumship, and psychic research. He and his brother, Peter, also wrote a book about ghosts and the history of ghost hunting.

When he was growing up, it wasn't *Boys' Life* and *Reader's Digest* resting on the coffee table, Aykroyd points out.

"*American Society for Psychical Research* journals were all around the house when I was a kid," he said. Those are heady paranormal research journals, in case you didn't know.

So when Aykroyd noticed the weird things happening around his house, his ghost-hunting instincts kicked in. First, the ghost would turn exercise equipment on. He said he also noticed that someone was moving jewelry on the dresser.

But that was just the start. The ghost, who apparently had few inhibitions, decided to climb into bed with the comedian one night. According to Aykroyd, he was dozing off and felt the bed depress next to him. For most people, sharing a bed with a spook would be too much. His reaction was different, though.

"I rolled over and just nuzzled up to whatever it was and went back to sleep."

Here is a man who is clearly at home—and even in bed—with the paranormal.

Aykroyd said he believed that it was Elliot's ghost that became his bedmate. He said the spirit just seemed big—and Elliot was a physically and spiritually big woman. So maybe Aykroyd, one of the world's great funny men and no stranger to practical jokes, was just kidding.

But what makes many people think that Aykroyd's story isn't just a leftover *Saturday Night Live* skit or a subplot from an upcoming *Ghostbusters* sequel is the fact that other people have had nearly the same encounter in the mansion. Not long after Aykroyd admitted to his supernatural run-ins with Elliot's ghost, another celebrity backed up his claim.

Actress Beverly D'Angelo, who owned the home before Aykroyd, went public in 2011 with her own paranormal encounters while filming a popular television show. She, too, thinks that Elliot may be the source of the haunting.

D'Angelo told her story on the Biography Channel's *Celebrity Ghost Stories*. The actress said that one night she had started to drift off to sleep when she heard a strange noise that, she guessed, was coming from the mantle. D'Angelo kept her jewelry and other small objects on the mantlepiece. She was meticulous about neatly stretching out her favorite pieces of jewelry across the flat surface of the mantle.

As she began to slip into a deeper sleep, D'Angelo said a swooshing sound roused her from unconsciousness. It was the distinct sound of metal sliding around, and it was coming from the mantle.

In the gray shadows of night, D'Angelo could see that the jewelry she had placed on the top of the mantle was moving from one side to the other. The pieces were also spinning and sliding along the surface of the mantle all by themselves.

There was no one around, and D'Angelo knew she was the only one in the room.

When one person says they witness a certain type of paranormal behavior, it's easy for skeptics to discount the story. There could be a natural explanation. The witness could be hallucinating. The witness could be lying. But when a few people come forward and claim they experienced similar paranormal activity in the same place at different times, the skeptics start to lose their edge in trying to prove the activity was fake or misinterpreted natural phenomena. Coincidences are rare events. Multiple coincidences are much rarer and typically reveal an underlying pattern, paranormal researchers point out.

In this case, strange behavior—jewelry moving—has been observed by at least two different homeowners at Elliot's mansion. Is that a coincidence, or a pattern?

Critics have one more complaint about the haunting at the mansion: Elliot didn't die in the mansion; she died in England. Skeptics wonder why she would haunt the mansion if she died a few thousand miles away. Eilfie Music, a paranormal researcher for the Paranormal Research Society and an original cast member of A&E's real-life drama *Paranormal State,* said that it's rare, but not unheard of, to have multiple sightings of the ghost of a single historical figure at different locations.

According to Music, although Elliot died in England, she may feel more attached to the mansion she lived in rather than a hotel room she was merely staying in during a tour.

Indeed, the rock and roll ghosts seem to hang out at more than one haunted site. The ghosts of Jim Morrison and Janis Joplin reportedly inhabit a few places, for example.

Music said the paranormal activity at Elliot's old mansion seems to be a mixture of residual and intelligent types of hauntings. In a residual haunting, the activity is almost like a spiritual tape recording that etches itself into the fabric of a location and gets repeated over and over again. An intelligent haunting suggests there is something—or someone—actively influencing and guiding the phenomena.

Cass—just like in life—seems to defy classification.

CHAPTER 10

GRAM PARSONS:

The Haunting of Room 8

Gram Parsons was used to rising from the ashes.

He was born into a wealthy family, but his childhood was a series of tragedies. When Parsons was twelve, his father committed suicide. His mother died of alcoholism on the day he graduated from high school. Parsons had the brains to go to Harvard, but he dropped out in the first semester.

Rising from the ashes, he became a rock star, playing in the band the Byrds and acquiring the reputation as a songwriter's songwriter from critics and colleagues. He helped form the Flying Burrito Brothers, a short-lived band that was the darling of rock and country critics all over the world.

Stardom did not sit well with Parsons, and he began to rebel. His family and friends could see the old flames of drug and alcohol abuse whipping up around him and threatening to envelop him. It wouldn't be the first time Parsons would seek solace in a bottle. It was the last, though. Parsons died of an overdose at the Joshua Tree Inn in California in 1973, just a few months shy of induction into rock's infamous 27 Club.

It's no wonder that visitors to that motel expect Parsons to rise from the ashes just one more time. Parsons loved the area. The musician, who most say created alternative country music, wrote songs about the canyons and desert that surround the little inn and provide a mystical, otherworldly vista for guests.

Parsons partied and even chased UFOs there, too.

The focus of the paranormal activity is in Room 8, where Parsons took his last breath. The room has become an attraction of sorts, catering to paranormal buffs looking for a place where they might run into a ghost or catch sight of a UFO. Then there are Parsons's fans who want a psychic brush with their hero.

Whatever their reasons, guests continue to stay in the room, and the rumors of apparitions and strange phenomena continue to filter in. While most people think that it's Parsons doing the haunting in the motel, others aren't so sure. It should be noted that Joshua Tree is an area that is full of haunted legends and tales. Finding a ghost in Joshua Tree is like shooting fish in a barrel.

Fans, however, are convinced that Parsons is haunting the motel. They say they can sense that Parsons is near, and at times they feel someone is watching them. But there are other, more physical reminders of a haunting that convince those who stay at the Joshua Tree Inn that Parsons is revisiting his old digs.

In the case of the haunted hotel room, shadows are seen sliding along the walls, but there are no solid objects casting these strange, dark masses. Guests also say that objects move as if they are being pushed by an unseen presence. This evidence points to an intelligent haunting in the motel room.

Paranormal researchers say an intelligent spirit can interact with the world of the living. It has a personality and can even respond to questions and commands.

Interestingly, a lot of people who have stayed in Room 8 say that a mirror is the focal point of the haunting there. Apparently, the mirror is one of the remaining pieces of furniture that would have been in the room at the time of Parsons's passing. Guests say that in the middle of the night, the mirror begins to move. They describe the movement as a swaying or rocking. It appears to be under intelligent control, like someone is pushing it. They also say that no one was walking around or moving in the room at the time they observed the phenomena.

Maybe it's natural seismic activity, some skeptics speculate, but none of the guests in other rooms of the motel report this type of activity. It's hard to imagine an earthquake localized in Room 8. Paranormally speaking, the haunted mirror has a precedent. In occult lore, mirrors are thought to be portals between dimensions or to the afterlife. Mediums are also known to tap the power of the mirror to predict the future.

Another explanation for Parsons's restless activity in the Joshua Tree Inn involves his odd burial.

Several accounts say that after Parsons died, his body was taken to a funeral home to be prepared for burial. His family wanted to bury him in Louisiana, but his friends believed their buddy would want to remain in California's Joshua Tree, the area he loved so much. They then did what any crazy friends of any crazy rock star would do: they stole the body and attempted to cremate it themselves. Commandeering a borrowed hearse, they drove to a spot in Joshua Tree National

Park called Cap Rock, poured gasoline into the opened coffin, and threw in a lit match.

What happened next was a scene that was one part Keystone Cops and one part rock and roll legend.

The huge fireball that appeared when the gasoline ignited happened to alert authorities, who were already looking for the body snatchers. The cops then gave chase to the would-be undertakers, who managed to temporarily escape. Later, the friends said that they were able to elude the cops because the police were encumbered by their own sobriety.

Parsons's friends remained at large for a short while, but the slow, sober police eventually caught up with them. The authorities were also able to rescue the burning body and later transported it to Louisiana, where it was finally buried.

Oftentimes, the failure to properly bury a body, or the burial of a body in a place against the wishes of the deceased, can set off a haunting. Parsons could be restless in death because of the burial hijinks. Then again, he may be restless because his friends were right—he wanted to remain in Joshua Tree.

Fans of the Byrds and of Parsons still make the journey to Joshua Tree Inn. The spot of his impromptu funeral has become a just-as-impromptu shrine, with fans leaving mementos and nicknacks celebrating Parsons's work and life. The National Park Service quickly cleans up any new tributes that are placed in the spot, though. A more permanent memorial was moved to the Joshua Tree Inn.

CHAPTER 11

BLACK SABBATH:

The Haunting of One of Metal's Darkest Bands

Geezer Butler, Black Sabbath's bassist and the band's most prolific lyricist, says that the only devils the band ever summoned were the suit-wearing, contract-wielding businessmen who made their careers a living hell during the pioneering heavy metal band's wild ride to fame, fortune, and wanton destruction during the late 1960s and early 1970s.

But Butler must have forgotten—or is repressing—the dark visitor that appeared at his bed one night following a disturbing nightmare that may have just been influenced by Butler's recent interest in black magic.

Butler was raised a Catholic, so the devil was not something new to the bassist. Butler, however, began to have a different relationship with the Lord of the Underworld later in life. While fans often tie Black Sabbath's macabre songs and stage performances to the group's lead singer, Ozzy Osbourne, Butler was arguably the brains behind the operation. His gift for words and penetrating inquisitiveness added depth and artistry to the group's sinister-sounding songs.

It was that inquisitiveness, Butler would say, that led him to the dark arts. Like Led Zeppelin's Jimmy Page, Butler was attracted to the writings of Aleister Crowley. He voraciously read Crowley's works and those of a number of other occult writers. Those occult themes were hugely influential as the band took shape. Fans find occult references on Black Sabbath's album covers and hear them in Black Sabbath's songs and, later, in Osbourne's own songs, like "Mr. Crowley."

Under the spell of Crowley and the occult, Black Sabbath began to transform. They were once a blues band called Earth. As their experimentation in the occult deepened, that bluesy, rootsy music was replaced by throbbing, edgy hard rock, and, of course, the band name was changed to a term synonymous with devil-worshipping rituals.

As the band began to explore the dark arts musically, Butler continued studying the occult, and it quickly took hold of the bassist's life. For instance, Butler's interior decorating style began to reflect his infernal, contemporary side. He painted his apartment black and added inverted crosses throughout it.

One day, as the band members began work on what would become their eponymous *Black Sabbath* album, Osbourne showed up with a book on sixteenth-century magic. The lead singer, who said he had stolen the book, knew that Butler was interested in ritual magic and offered the book as a gift to his friend.

Butler immediately found a place for the ancient tome in a cupboard.

That night, Butler said he had a fitful night's sleep. He eventually drifted off, but suddenly awoke. At the foot of his bed, Butler said he saw something that he could only describe as an inky black shadow. He said he could only see the shape because it was actually darker than the night. That's really dark.

Whatever this presence was, it infused the room with a nasty vibe. Butler felt like the room was radiating dread. The spirit didn't move. It seemed to stare at the bassist for a few moments, and then—without reason or urging—instantly vanished. For Butler, seeing the devil was not as fun as writing songs about him.

"It was a horrible presence that frightened the life out of me!" Butler would later comment.

He immediately went to the cupboard and tossed the book into the trash. While the bassist never saw the shadow creature again, the strange magic continued to haunt the band—sometimes for good and sometimes for bad.

Ozzy said one of the more positive encounters with whatever spirits were haunting the band began when an early lineup of the group met to rehearse and record a song. Butler and guitarist Tony Iommi started to play riffs for Ozzy—and ended up playing the exact same riff at the exact same time. They were playing the same notes at the same rhythm and tempo, too.

Neither musician had heard the tune before. It just sort of appeared out of thin air into both of the musicians' brains and hands. Butler immediately sensed that some type of force was guiding them. Legend has it that he named the song—and the band—Black Sabbath right after the riff-synchronicity incident.

In another case, Black Sabbath gets the rap for stirring up an evil entity that was bent on destroying a California family in the 1970s.

You may have watched the 1981 movie *The Entity*, which was a huge hit starring Barbara Hershey, but you may not have known that it was based on actual events. The real entity case was investigated by pioneering parapsychologist Dr. Barry E. Taff, who wrote about the incident in his book *Aliens Above, Ghosts Below*. The book is a serious ride into the unknown from one of the legends in the paranormal research community.

Taff writes that he originally heard about the case that would eventually inspire the movie from an associate. The fellow paranormal investigator was talking about a haunted house with a friend at a bookstore. While the two paranormal investigators chatted, Doris Bithers, a single mother, approached Taff's associate and said that her home, too, was haunted. She told them about some of the incidents she and her family had experienced after moving into the small house.

The word "experienced" might be too tame to describe the haunting.

In fact, as the victim began to fill the investigators in on the haunting, the details were so mind-blowing that even this group of open-minded paranormal experts found them unbelievable. Bithers said that not only was her home haunted, but the spirits—or whatever was in the house—were also physically attacking her. Even worse, they were sexually assaulting her. After the associate passed on the information to Taff about the strange phenomena in the home, the team decided to investigate.

The actual encounters between the entity and Doris and her four children in their California home were not quite as spectacular as the Hollywood version of events, but the evidence collected by the team of investigators and the activities they observed there went well beyond the phenomena that most paranormal investigators endure. During their study, the group witnessed a range of anomalous activities, from horrible smells that had no discernible source to odd photographic effects, including the bleaching out of certain figures in photos.

But it was the odd light effects that Taff observed that piqued his curiosity and prompted further investigation. The lights were more than just mere flashes. They were three-dimensional, with the ability to change colors. Weirder still, they seemed to respond to the team.

One of the sons noted that the spirits that were running the odd light show responded dramatically when he played heavy metal songs, especially Black Sabbath and Uriah Heep tunes. Taff, indeed, saw the light activity increase considerably when the team played the songs.

"Much to our surprise," Taff writes, "when the records were playing the songs indicated by Doris's son, the anomalous light activity increased dramatically, reaching a crescendo in conjunction with the music, in fact, with specific passages within each of the two songs."

In an e-mail interview, Taff said that he could not remember the exact passages of the songs that boosted the activity. The case is more than thirty-nine years old, and some of the details can no longer be recalled by the witnesses and investigators. Doris and her sons were convinced that the home was haunted by a demon or the devil himself. The music was charging up the spirits, in their opinion.

Taff wasn't so sure. He wondered whether the fast-tempo, loud-volume music wasn't physically altering the space and creating changes to the lights. Or perhaps the music was affecting the witnesses, who were using a form of psychokinesis to alter the light patterns.

Over a period of a few weeks, the group experienced more and more bizarre activity in the home. The investigators installed large poster boards on the windows to ensure that outside lights weren't creating the anomalous lights inside.

Bithers reported that the panels were being ripped down. During one seance, Taff said they saw the poster boards fall away from the windows. It wasn't like the panels became unglued and gradually fell naturally. The motion was violent, like unseen hands were tearing them from the walls.

It's easy to have 20/20 vision looking back thirty-nine years after the event, but maybe they should have pasted some Black Sabbath posters on the windows instead?

CHAPTER 12

EDDIE HINTON:
Picking and Haunting

Muscle Shoals, Alabama, in case you don't know, is primarily known for two things:

One: Hard-living, hard-drinking, brilliant musicians. Eddie Hinton fit that description.

Two: Ghosts. Hinton fits that description, too.

Not too many people know about Hinton, and that's a shame. He was a master guitar player, shredding lead guitar for the famous Muscle Shoals Sound Rhythm Section from 1967 to 1971. While known primarily as one of the great guitar players of the area, he was also a soulful singer. He was good enough to get noticed by some of the greats. Stars like Wilson Pickett, Aretha Franklin, Percy Sledge, and even Elvis Presley clamored to have Hinton play on their albums and in their bands.

But Hinton was more than just a session player, more than a great singer. He was a triple threat. Hinton's songwriting skills were unmatched, even among the topflight musicians in one of the South's most musical areas. As proof, both Dusty Springfield and Chrissie Hynde recorded his song "Breakfast in Bed."

What strikes most people about a Hinton song isn't the incredible soul of the song—that was kind of expected among Muscle Shoals musicians. What makes Hinton's songs stand out is the sensitivity.

In a 2005 thread on an Allman Brothers Band fan site, Jim Dickinson, a Memphis music producer, said, "I never saw more talent in any one person than Eddie Hinton had."

When Hinton was gigging in the Muscle Shoals area, he was usually referred to as "the next big thing." Most people thought it was just a matter of time before Hinton made it big.

But that wasn't to be.

Eddie led a volatile life, and he passed away at age fifty-one after suffering a heart attack. Though Hinton released some albums that created a cult following for the musician, he died before his presence could be felt by a mass audience. But his presence is still felt in other ways.

That leads us to the other thing that people find in the Muscle Shoals area. The Shoals has its share of ghosts and haunted spots. Hinton's intensity burned like a supernova, and when he finally passed on, that light didn't fade. It exploded. As we've seen in other cases, big personalities and unfinished business typically add up to a great rock and roll ghost story.

Ghost hunters and paranormal experts say that an intense personality like Hinton's may have made it difficult for his spirit to cross to the other side, and, like a star that never quite reached its zenith, the spirit of one of Muscle Shoal's forgotten stars may still feel he has something left to accomplish here on earth.

Indeed, there are stories that the musician's spirit is still hanging out, waiting for his chance to shine. Several musicians have said they saw Eddie hanging out at the Muscle Shoals Sound Studio, where the Muscle Shoals sound was defined and where the Rolling Stones cut the classic tune "Wild Horses."

A couple musicians told friends that they saw a man in a blue suit in the studio. The figure appeared suddenly and wandered around. Then poof, he was gone. Initially, the musicians thought he was just another studio player or an employee, except he was dressed a little, let's say, out of date. And there wasn't supposed to be anyone else in the studio at the time.

It gets creepier. When the witnesses described the peculiar clothes the man was wearing—particularly the blue suit—to some people who were familiar with Hinton and his wandering spirit, they realized the musicians were talking about the same suit that Eddie Hinton was buried in. Obviously, these folks hadn't been at Eddie's funeral. They would have had no way of knowing what Eddie was wearing in his casket.

The shadowy figure that moved through the studios also matched the description of the size and shape of the legendary Muscle Shoals musician. Eddie always enjoyed the company of musicians, and he apparently still likes to hang out with them.

Not all of the musicians who have cut an album in Muscle Shoals have seen Eddie's ghost. But a few musicians who traveled to Alabama have said they felt Eddie's presence in other ways. The Black Keys, like a lot of bands who hope the Muscle

Shoals recording magic will rub off on their artistic creations, traveled to the area to record an album. Weird things were waiting for them. The band's engineer said that a string of incidents convinced him that it was more than bad luck affecting the equipment. Microphones burned out, and lights would blink on and off.

His explanation: ghosts.

Maybe Eddie was just bummed out that the band didn't ask him to sit in on the session.

Another picker, Richard Young of the Kentucky Headhunters, had his own encounter with Eddie's spirit. While recording the album *Soul* and seeking to deepen his already substantial Southern rock roots, Richard unexpectedly encountered the spirit of Eddie Hinton. At a point of creative confusion for Richard, a new acquaintance passed on a cut of Eddie's song "Dear Y'all." It worked, Richard said in an interview on Swampland.com, and he credit's Eddie's influence—or spirit:

> I don't know how I had missed out on it, but that album did more to fire me up to do whatever it was that I brought to that band on this album than anything! I would not have been able to do it without Eddie Hinton. It was like his ghost was present. It reinstated my faith that a white boy has got soul too.

Then again, it may have been the soul of a white boy—named Eddie Hinton—that reinstated his faith in music.

CHAPTER 13

SID AND NANCY:

The Spirit of Punk Lives On

To say there's weird activity going on at the Chelsea Hotel in New York City is an understatement. There's definitely weird stuff going on at all times at one of the city's most famous rock and roll hotels.

The question is, how much of the weird stuff that goes on there is actually paranormal?

The 250-unit hotel, which is located on Twenty-third Street in the Chelsea neighborhood of Manhattan, has served as a roost for numerous bohemians of all artforms—writers, artists, and musicians. It's infamous, however, as the scene of one of the most brutal crimes in rock and roll history: the stabbing and death of Nancy Spungen, the girlfriend of punk rock star Sid Vicious.

Police say that on October 12, 1978, Spungen was found dead in her room from a single stab wound. They traced the murder weapon back to Vicious, the former bassist for the Sex

Pistols. Vicious was arrested, but died of a heroin overdose while out on bail.

"I'll die before I'm twenty-five, and when I do I'll have lived the way I wanted to," Vicious said prophetically in a 1977 interview with the *Daily Mirror*.

Since his death and Spungen's murder, rumors have circulated that the spirits of Sid and Nancy have joined the hotel's extensive guest list of haunted inhabitants. For decades, the Chelsea Hotel has been a prime location for people looking for ghosts and spirits, but guests say that after punk rock's most infamous murder-suicide, the hotel must have made sure that one more room was available for Spungen and Vicious because the haunted activity in the hotel has intensified.

The hotel keeps good records of its paranormal residents and encourages its mortal guests to report any spooky run-ins or incidents. Several of the more recent accounts seem to be centered on Sid and Nancy.

One former guest at the hotel named Matt wrote that he and a friend stayed in Room 124, not too far from Room 100, where the murder took place. They liked the room, but noticed that the couch looked strange. The friends joked that it looked like it had been taken from on old funeral parlor. They even snapped pictures of each other on the couch posing as dead people. Probably not a good thing to do in a haunted hotel.

After a night of touring the city, the two friends returned to their room and were talking. Matt said his friend was sitting on the creepy-looking couch when he turned as white as, well, a ghost. The friend then said, matter-of-factly, "I just saw a ghost."

A "fuzzy" image of a man walked out of the hotel room's bathroom and disappeared, he said.

Matt, who had been known to joke around, figured his friend was just pulling his leg, but the friend continued to tell him that he had seen a ghost and that he wanted to delete the pictures they had taken earlier. He sensed there was something bad that had happened on the couch and that it was wrong to make light of the tragedy. Not used to seeing his friend this distraught, Matt began to take him more seriously.

It wasn't their last run-in with the spiritual forces in the hotel room.

A few minutes later, Matt felt a strange force next to him in the bathroom. He struggled to describe the force. It wasn't static electricity. It was different. The situation grew more intense and violent. Something began pulling out a few hairs on his right forearm. He quickly scanned the room for an explanation. There were no drafts, and no one else was in the room.

After the two guests discussed the incident, the friend told Matt that he believed they had made contact with the ghost of Vicious. They may have even called him up from the beyond. He reminded Matt that the two had been playing a few of Sid Vicious and the Sex Pistol's songs. Maybe playing the tunes had summoned the punk rocker's ghost.

Another guest commented that he and a friend had stayed in Room 124 and had a similar eerie feeling there. They also claimed to have seen a filmy object that looked like a disembodied hand move along the staircase of the hotel. The two felt that some of the activity had been worse when they sat on the couch in the room.

Did these guests come in contact with the presence of Sid Vicious, too?

Other guests have not just felt the presence, they've heard it. Once, a hotel guest on the first floor received an urgent call from a friend staying on the ninth floor. The friend thought someone had stolen her passport. She then said that the room seemed like it was going crazy, too. The lights and television were on when she went into the room, and she was sure she had turned them off. Then, suddenly, the television turned on and off by itself.

The guest raced to the ninth floor as quickly as possible to help her friend.

They eventually found the passport, but their problems in the haunted hotel weren't over. No sooner did the emotions start to die down than the pair heard the moan of a female. The moan became a scream, like someone was being murdered.

The rest of the night, the friends were completely unnerved.

But they made it to checkout time.

After that fitful night of sleep and worry, they decided to film the hotel lobby. When they played the video back, a male voice groaned over the audio. Neither guest could remember hearing the sound when they were filming. They couldn't remember anyone standing nearby when they shot the video. The friends reasoned that if someone had been close enough to make that noise, they certainly would have appeared in the video. But there was no one on the video who could have made the groan that was picked up on the camera's microphone.

A lot of ghost hunters and paranormal researchers wonder whether the horrifying murder of Nancy Spungen, or Sid Vicious's untimely death, carved itself into the supernatural fiber of the Chelsea Hotel, and this is what these guests are experiencing. But others are not so sure. The hotel is so haunted that many of those familiar with the Chelsea Hotel haunting believe it would be impossible to identify the living beings that are behind the ghostly occurrences.

Those hoping to get a room at the Chelsea to investigate the ghosts of Sid and Nancy for themselves might be disappointed. As of the time of publication of this book, the hotel has closed for restoration and there are rumors that the hotel may be converted into a condominium or apartment complex.

CHAPTER 14

KURT COBAIN:

Of Grunge and Ghosts

Kurt Cobain tapped into the veins of disillusionment and angst of Generation X like no one else during the 1990s. As frontman for the band Nirvana, he was the crown prince of grunge music, a Seattle-based, flannel-draped version of punk rock that spread out of the Northwest and became a global music phenomenon.

Other bands, like Pearl Jam and Soundgarden, soon carried the banner of the Seattle sound, which became a genuine musical phenomenon that ranks right up there with some other geographically centered rock styles, like the Mersey sound and the Athens sound.

But Cobain wasn't so much a rock star as he was a rock sore.

His music—angry, painful, and sullen—wasn't some kind of fluke, or an act. It matched his spirit, note for note, scar for scar. The wealth and fame that often satisfy the darker spirits of rock stars who finally attain superstardom seemed to make

Cobain's spirit even darker and angrier. He struggled with and escaped substance abuse and then fell back into abusing harder drugs. His binges were legendary, and some of his friends suggested that Cobain was suicidal.

He drifted in and out of rehab and treatment centers. In early April of 1994, he walked out of one final rehab and went missing. His wife, Courtney Love, hired a private detective to find him, according to some stories.

As the hours passed, friends and family members grew more concerned that something horrible had happened to Cobain.

On April 8, 1994, an electrician found the body of the Nirvana frontman in a greenhouse on Cobain's property. He had a gunshot wound to the head, and a suicide note was found near the body.

In a quote attributed to Cobain, the musician reportedly said: "If you die, you're completely happy and your soul somewhere lives on. I'm not afraid of dying. Total peace after death, becoming someone else, is the best hope I've got."

That statement seemed to predict Cobain's sudden and tragic death as well as his new journeys in the spirit world, because it wasn't too long after Cobain's death that ghost stories about him began to filter in. The stories seem to be focused on a park—called Viretta Park—right outside of Cobain's home. It's a small park, just a little under two acres. We can narrow down the activity even more—most of the sightings take place on a bench in that park. Several witnesses reported they saw Cobain on the bench just a few hours before he died.

After his death, the park bench became a makeshift memorial for fans of Nirvana and Cobain. Fans stop by and drop off a cigarette for Cobain, or write a message on the bench. They jot down their favorite Nirvana lyrics or Cobain quotes on it as well. On certain anniversaries, such as the anniversary of Cobain's death, fans gather at the bench to remember the singer.

Since Cobain's death, people have reported seeing the lonesome figure of a young man sitting on the bench. The figure looks a lot like him. Others say they have seen anomalous lights in the park and around the bench.

Paranormal researchers say that it might not be Cobain's ghost that is the cause of the strange lights and images near the bench at all, but that the area has become paranormally active because it is a focal point of the psychic energy given off by fans. All that grief and emotion collects as energy and manifests in anomalous activity—like strange lights and orbs, as well as spirit sightings. If that's the case, it may be the fans that are haunting the site, not Cobain.

But it doesn't seem like Cobain, who was a wanderer, to have his spirit stuck in one place. Fans from all over the world have reported receiving visits from Cobain's spirit and have started to post the details of these supernatural run-ins on Internet websites and message boards. Some are farfetched. One woman claims that Cobain appeared to her on the screen of her computer and asked her to give him a kiss. As she did, Cobain disappeared.

Other reports are more plausible, in a paranormal sense. One writer—who doesn't seem to be an obsessed Nirvana fan—said that he saw the figure of a young man appear in his bedroom. He said the ghost had straggly brown hair and wore old clothes and a flannel shirt. He seemed to be in his mid to late twenties, a good description of Cobain's age when he died—yep, another member of the 27 Club. The writer's sister said the description sounded a lot like Kurt Cobain, so he nicknamed the spirit "Kurt." The spirit was neither transparent nor solid, but something in between. That's an apt description for a spirit trying to pass on to the other side, too.

The ghost eventually went away.

Of course, there's no telling whether the ghost in the teen's room was actually Cobain's spirit or maybe the ghost of some look-alike. It may be easy to be a Cobain look-alike spirit, but it's much harder to be a sound-alike.

Our next story indicates that Cobain may be gone, but he is still in the recording business. One paranormal researcher believes he may have contacted Cobain using a controversial technology called a ghost box. The ghost box randomly cycles through radio channels and spits out bursts of words and music. It's a relatively new invention used by some paranormal researchers, although most still use their trusty Ouija boards and automatic-writing utensils to talk with ghosts.

Believers in the ghost box insist that if you listen closely to the device, disembodied spirits will communicate, shaping these bursts of noise into messages that they want to pass on to the living. The device operates somewhat like an electronic version of the Ouija board. A person asks a question and then listens to any potential messages.

In this case, the researcher had apparently been asked by a friend to use the ghost box to contact Cobain. The researcher announced his intention to talk with Cobain. A few seconds later, the name Kurt Cobain erupted out of the random blanket of noise. Most fans agree that it not only sounds like someone is pronouncing the words "Kurt Cobain," but it sounds like it is actually Cobain's voice saying his name.

It may be that Kurt, for all his disappointment and disillusion with stardom, may still be reaching out to his fans from the grave.

CHAPTER 15

MICHAEL JACKSON:

The Thriller Turns Chiller

He was the king of pop.

His 1982 album *Thriller* lived up to its name by breaking just about every music industry sales record in history—records that will likely never be topped again. Jackson was one of those artists who could do it all. He wrote his own songs. He could dance. Nearly every human being who lived at the height of Jacksonmania did his famous "moonwalk," or at least tried to do the step.

He also acted. Choreographed. Invested.

You name it and Michael Jackson did it.

Meanwhile, the Jackson empire was raking in millions.

Born into a working showbiz family, Michael Jackson had a career that spanned decades. That nearly five-decade-long career started in the hardscrabble streets of Gary, Indiana, where he was a child prodigy groomed to be the star in the midst of his four musical brothers who made up the 1970s supergroup the Jackson Five. That career ended, tragically, in his home in Los Angeles, California, on June 25, 2009, amidst a swirl of rumors of drug abuse and dependency. Jackson's bizarre lifestyle was the stuff of tabloid legend for decades, and there were many who suggested that his odd habits and behavior finally caught up with him.

Jackson's story has all the ingredients of a rock and roll ghost story. We have a celebrity—full of equal parts tragedy and promise—who finds it difficult to transition off the mortal stage, and we have a rabid fanbase that's unwilling to let their favorite star rest in peace. In fact, Jackson's death brought scads of reports that the singer may no longer be just thrilling fans, but chilling them to the core.

The news of Jackson's death had no sooner started to spread when fans began to experience paranormal events that ranged from the goofy to the terrifying. Witnesses said they saw spirits near places that were connected to Jackson's death—around his home, at Neverland Ranch, and near the Ronald Reagan UCLA Medical Center, where Jackson was pronounced dead. They even took pictures, which made their rounds on the Internet, along with rumors that those photos were faked, or staged, or simply misidentified natural phenomena.

You would expect weird things to happen to the departed spirit of the man who once had a chimp for a best friend and lived in an amusement park. But things got even weirder for the departed King of Pop.

The first bizarre incident occurred during the taping of interviews for *Larry King Live* at Jackson's Neverland Ranch. The property had special significance for Jackson. At the height of his fame, he bought the ranch and turned it into a Disneyland away from Disneyland, complete with tree houses, a zoo, and amusement rides.

As thousands of fans watched the broadcast, they noticed a figure glide past one of the walls as Larry King and his crew conducted interviews. Hardcore fans believed—and still believe—that the figure was the ghost of Jackson. The production company quickly explained the event away, saying it was just a member of the crew who walked past a light and cast a shadow on the wall.

Other reports of Jackson ghost sightings flooded in.

During a *Today Show* interview of Jackson's brother Jermaine, fans say they saw Michael looking out on the garden as his brother spoke. Jermaine has not commented on the sighting, but he has been public about his belief in the paranormal and ghosts.

Michael's sister La Toya has also gone public with ghostly encounters with her brother. She said he still visits her home. When she walks around, she can feel Michael's presence. Initially, she thought that only she could sense the presence—possibly just her imagination trying to compensate for the loss of her brother. But then a security guard mentioned that he felt a presence in the home at times. The dog began to bark at Michael's old room, like there was an intruder. At times, La Toya heard someone tap dancing upstairs, just like she and her brother used to do every Sunday.

"It's the strangest thing because you feel something, like, thick around you or behind you and you're wondering—you don't see anything, but you feel a presence… It's very interesting because it's there, it's definitely there," La Toya said in a story on Radar Online.

Neighbors of Jackson's home in L.A.—the one where he took his final breath—are among those who say Jackson hasn't beat it at all. And they're pretty freaked out about it.

The neighbors say that at times they can hear Jackson singing. They check to see if there are fans or practical jokers hanging around the mansion, but no one is there. Music also seeps out of the home at odd hours, raising suspicion from those who live nearby that Jackson's ghost is haunting the mansion.

Will.i.am, a member of the band the Black Eyed Peas and a music producer who collaborated with Jackson, probably wouldn't find it difficult to believe that the pop star is still singing at his old digs. He's convinced that his own home recording studio is haunted by Jackson, according to friends. The producer hasn't worked in the studio since Jackson's death, preferring to work out his tunes on a little laptop computer.

It seems the child star who became one of the biggest stars in pop history isn't leaving the stage quite yet, and knowing Michael, each appearance will be bigger and better than the one before.

They don't call Jackson the Thriller for nothing.

CHAPTER 16

WHITNEY HOUSTON AND AMY WINEHOUSE:

There's No Die in Diva

There are a lot of ghost stories about rock stars who passed away decades ago—Elvis, John Lennon, Janis Joplin, etc. I know what you're thinking: but people were more superstitious then. No one believes that sort of thing anymore. But that's where you're wrong. Like some kind of paranormal Motown cranking out ghost story after ghost story, the haunted hits just keep on coming.

The latest tales are about two of the most popular female singers in the last decade or so, who had voices like angels. They also had inner demons that played a role in their untimely deaths, which may be one reason why these divas seem so intent on remaining in the world of mortals. Friends and family say that even today, the spirits of these songstresses are reaching out to friends and family members from the grave.

Whitney Houston, the talented and beautiful daughter of Cissy Houston and the cousin of Dionne Warwick, exploded on the 1980s music scene, earning platinum and double platinum albums, as her voice dazzled the critics.

To fans, the singer lived a charmed life. A triple threat, Whitney was also a model and an actress with modeling contracts and movie deals rolling in, bringing her more money and more fame. Her love life was full, too. She dated professional football star Randall Cunningham and comedian Eddie Murphy, just to name a few famous beaus.

But that image took a severe turn in 1992, when she married bad boy rhythm and blues singer Bobby Brown and a reality show exposed her bizarre lifestyle that, most guessed, was fueled by substance abuse.

Despite a few attempted comebacks, Whitney's music-filled life ended abruptly in a hotel on February 9, 2012. Her friends, family, and fans were distraught when they heard the news that she had died. When pressed, though, most weren't surprised.

Just like in the aftermath of Michael Jackson's death, ghost stories immediately started to circulate.

Bobbi Kristina, Whitney's daughter, was, obviously, particularly hard hit by her mother's death, but she told Oprah Winfrey that she believed her mother was reaching out to her from beyond. Bobbi Kristina said that lights in her home would turn on and off without explanation. She had her own explanation, though. She believed that her mother was causing the light show, trying to signal her presence to her daughter. Bobbi Kristina also believed that her mother was attempting to contact her in other ways. She said that she can sometimes hear her mother speak to her—telling her to keep going on with her life. The star's daughter said that on a few occasions she could even feel the spirit of Whitney Houston pass through her body.

Bobbi Kristina told another story about her mother's continued contact. She said that Whitney passed down a family legend that the saints wake up at 5:00 a.m. to pray. After her mother's death, Bobbi Kristina would, inexplicably, wake up night after night at 5:00 a.m.

Skeptics would say that these accounts are either coincidence or the result of a grieving young lady, but there are other friends and family members who have experienced an encounter with the spirit of the singer, including Whitney's mother. Cissy Houston, who was unable to speak at her daughter's funeral due to grief, wrote a letter that said Whitney's spirit had communicated to her in a strange way that she had passed on.

According to Cissy, the day that Whitney's body was discovered, she heard the doorbell ring. She called the concierge and asked him who was ringing the bell. The concierge checked the video cameras and could see that nobody was there. Cissy was convinced that either her daughter's spirit was reaching out to her, or God was trying to warn her that something was wrong.

It wasn't just family members who said that they had experienced a connection with the departed spirit of Whitney Houston. Fans began to report anomalies as they gathered around the spot where she died and at her funeral. Some had photographic evidence, posting pictures of orbs surrounding the ambulance transporting Whitney's body and hovering outside of the window of her hotel room.

Were they just photographic glitches? Were they due to odd atmospheric conditions?

Maybe, but lots of fans would suggest that a spirit as large as Whitney's would not fade slowly into the shadow world beyond, but would burn just as brightly as she made her transition from this world to the next.

Ghost Lady Sings the Blues

Amy Winehouse had a voice that was as biting as Whitney Houston's was soothing, and as real as Whitney's was astral, but the singers' spirits were similar. They both had a desire to create great music. They both were considered the best vocalists in their genres. And they both apparently clung to their earthly existences long after their mortal shells were shed.

Winehouse was a force, as industry insiders would say. For a tiny English girl, she belted out the blues and soul like any one of the famous songsmiths on her list of influences, from Billie Holiday to Otis Redding to the Shangri-las. Her career was one of those twisted catch-22s. When pressed, most friends admit her inner demons fueled her musical explorations, but they also fueled her descent into drugs, alcohol, and—some would say—madness.

On July 23, 2011, that descent finally hit bottom, and another member of rock's 27 Club officially checked in. She died—like Jimi and Janis and so many other hard-living rock and rollers—at the age of twenty-seven.

But Winehouse, who scored her biggest hit with "Rehab," a song about refusing help for drug and alcohol abuse, wasn't quite ready to completely stop performing, some of her friends said. They believe that her spirit has made contact with them from the other side—and it's not always a joyous reunion. According to reports in Britain's newspaper *The Sun*, one believer is her former boyfriend and often partner-in-crime, Pete Doherty.

Doherty told friends he left his home in London because he was continually seeing the ghost of his former girlfriend. He saw Amy's spirit not once, but four times, he explained to friends. Her image would suddenly appear in reflections in windows around the home, according to newspaper accounts. Doherty became so scared that he fled the country and traveled to France. There were reports that even before her death, Winehouse felt there were demons and negative energy in the London home. That may lend credence to Winehouse's ex-boyfriend's story.

Other friends believe that Doherty's vision was a result of drugs and maybe guilt for his enablement of Winehouse's self-destructive personality. However, the rocker claims to be clean and sober.

The truth is, Doherty isn't the only one who has had a paranormal encounter with the singer. A slew of psychic mediums have reportedly made contact with Winehouse. One medium said she received a message that the singer wanted to pass on: she was at peace—finally—and with her grandmother.

Since her passing, reports of ghostly encounters with Winehouse have gradually diminished. Maybe the psychic is right and she is ready to pass on. Her fans hope that wherever she is, she's finally at peace.

SECTION II

HAUNTED STUDIOS AND CONCERT VENUES

Just as all the great religions build majestic temples, members of royalty build ornate castles, and governments build massive town halls, the music industry has created its own sacred sites. These special spots are places where music is created and where musicians connect with live audiences.

In this section, we'll visit some of rock's most famous supernatural sites: recording studios, rock clubs and bars, concert halls, and other venues. Paranormal experts say these spots are like spirit sponges, soaking up the creative energy of rock stars and turning it into supernatural activity.

Like alchemists toiling in electronic laboratories, artists and producers enter recording studios, turning tape and wax and now digital files into gold and platinum. Studios are places where music history is made and where culture is changed. The names of the bands and singers that recorded million-selling monster hits are now enshrined in rock history and the Rock and Roll Hall of Fame, but some of these studios have become just as equally well known as the careers and the songs that were created in them.

Electric Ladyland.

Abbey Road.

Sun Studios.

Those are just a few of the recording studios that have entered the lexicon of rock history.

But there are other studios that have become famous for another, darker reason: they're haunted. In the ghostlore that surrounds rock and roll, studios are like haunted mansions: dark, quiet spaces that are filled with spirits and mysteries.

It's a matter of conjecture why ghosts seem to attach themselves to studios. Maybe it's the psychic activity that surrounds the artistic process. Musicians and producers usually have huge personalities and unquenchable imaginations. Maybe this power filters into the fabric of the studio, causing all types of anomalous activity, like outbreaks of poltergeist activity. After all, people have used music as a way to commune with the spirits and the gods for thousands of years. Anthropologists believe that is one reason why music was created in the first place.

Paranormal researchers also suggest that residual spirits are more likely to find a home in a studio. Residual hauntings are caused when extremely tragic and emotional events occur, and, like a tape getting stuck in an endless loop, the event repeats itself in space and time, over and over. These researchers also suggest that people can see, hear, and sometimes even smell this residual energy.

It would make sense that creating a work of art—like a song, or a collection of songs—would rev up both the creative juices and the creative tensions. That emotion, then, would be etched into the very fiber of space-time itself and serve as a basis for this type of residual experience.

Other theories indicate that the artists themselves may be the source of the hauntings. Paranormal researchers suggest that the creative powers of these musicians are stronger than they thought and that they tap into dimensions they could barely imagine. The strange phenomena that accompany poltergeist hauntings—like objects that move by themselves and lights and electronic equipment that turn on and off spontaneously—appear to arise from the consciousness of a troubled or agitated soul, often referred to in poltergeist lore as the "agent."

Taking this theory into the studio, we could imagine that artists, who are often young and tempestuous souls, may produce supernatural effects on the environment around them.

So it might be that the studios themselves are not so special at all. These facilities, like thousands of other places, just happen to be located at the wrong supernatural place—or the right place, depending on your desire to run into spirits. The ghosts that haunt studios may have taken up residence long before the buildings were converted into hit-making factories.

Ghosts, it seems, don't seem to care whether the "Quiet Please! Recording" red light is on or not.

There are other spots where music magic happens—and ghosts seem to follow. Clubs and concert halls have been the settings for some of rock and roll's history-making shows. Think about Elvis performing live on the *Ed Sullivan Show*, or Jimi Hendrix sacrificing his guitar at the Monterey Pop Festival, or the Beatles playing the London Palladium, or Led Zeppelin riveting the crowd at Madison Square Garden.

These concerts blew away the audiences, like a volcanic eruption. The performances exploded into pop culture to become defining moments of their respective generations.

But giant concert halls and stadiums aren't the only places where rock history has been made. It's the small blues clubs, juke joints, bars, and dives that shaped the music and the musicians. These music venues also have a reputation for paranormal activity.

In this section, we'll travel to some of the most haunted clubs and the most paranormally charged concert venues in the world, and I'll leave it up to you to decide whether these sites are especially attractive to spirits, or just spots where, perhaps, artistic imagination goes a little overboard.

CHAPTER 17

ROBERT LANG STUDIOS:

The Spirits of the Seattle Sound

In the late 1980s and early 1990s, the northwestern United States was a sleepy artist enclave that attracted a group of rockers who wanted to do their own thing. The music they created was largely ignored by record executives, who thought of the bands in Seattle, Washington, and Portland, Oregon, as mere shadows in the spotlight glare cast by the bright lights and big hair of Los Angeles's heavy metal glam rock scene.

No one paid much attention to bands from Seattle and Portland.

But that was about to change, thanks to guys like Robert Lang and other musical pioneers who sensed something special about the music creeping out of bars and clubs in the Northwest. Groups like Nirvana and Pearl Jam were gigging around the Seattle area, gaining skill and perfecting their sound—a raw, biting music that seemed to be the antithesis of everything the major markets—places like L.A. and New York City—seemed interested in at the time.

Some called the music "grunge," a word that also aptly described the clothes and the living conditions of these bands. Shedding the made-up, leathered-up image of their contemporaries, grunge rockers wore flannel shirts and jeans from secondhand clothing stores. There was no mascara and eyeliner. Their hair didn't need volumizer.

As these bands began to look for places to record, many were drawn to an odd, multi-layered brick home in the Seattle suburbs. As they recorded at Robert Lang Studios, they became aware that they weren't the only ones who were attracted to this studio. It just so happens that the studio that became the artistic hub of Seattle's grunge scene also became known as a center of ghostly activity. Over the years, reports of bizarre electronic phenomena, gear glitches, and—spookiest of all—actual apparitions have filtered out of one of Seattle's most famous studios.

Robert Lang, the owner of the studio, doesn't shy from the rumors that the building is haunted. In fact, he's pretty sure the ghost is a buddy of his. In a magazine article, Lang talks about a friend and, basically, co-founder of the studio, whom everyone called "Dubby."

Dubby had a colorful past, Lang said, as he began to discover when the two met in the 1970s. Dubby had drifted from unusual job to unusual job, even working as a yacht captain. He also told tales that his dad was once a bootlegger and had amassed a small fortune.

The mysterious friend mentioned that he had buried money that he was going to use to help the partners build a bigger, better studio. Lang and Dubby were like long-lost brothers and shared a dream of moving Robert Lang Studios out of the smallish digs and into a bigger, hipper, and more modern facility. But the cost of either relocation or renovation—hundreds of thousands of dollars—stood in the way of that dream.

Dubby lived his life more like a rock star than most of the actual rock stars who recorded at the studio, according to Dubby's friends. But as is the case with a lot of fast-living rock stars, those excesses caught up with him. Dubby died, some said, after one of those characteristic hardcore binges.

Lang was inconsolable when he found out.

He never forgot his friend. Sometimes he would remember something his buddy said or did, and inevitably the thought of Dubby's buried treasure would swirl around in Lang's mind, almost as if the departed Dubby was prompting him to start his search.

And Lang did. At first, he bought a metal detector and scoured a nearby lot, trying to find a signal that the buried treasure was located in the lot.

Nothing.

Perhaps that wasn't Dubby's style. Instead, Lang, driven by an act of faith, began to dig into the foundation of his studio. The operation lasted for months, but something kept driving Lang to finish the project.

One day, as Lang toiled, his shovel hit something hard where there shouldn't have been a solid object. He described that moment to the magazine:

> It was pouring down rain and I had this little orange trouble light hanging on the sewer line. I'm digging on the north side of the plot, and the sand sloughs. All of a sudden appears this big plastic canister, just the edge of it. I'll never forget this: I looked at it and time just stopped.

He looked in the canister and found $100 bills, and while he didn't reveal exactly how many bills, he said, "It was a lot of money."

It was almost like Dubby had reached beyond the grave, opened up his wallet, and bestowed a financial blessing on his friend to help him pay for the move to a new, state-of-the-art studio.

Or was it Dubby's way of paying a share of the rent? Because, according to Lang and dozens of other witnesses, the old yacht captain and regional man of mystery wasn't one to abandon his friends. They say Dubby is still hanging around.

In fact, Lang says Dubby hasn't just revealed himself to a few of the former employees and engineers at Robert Lang Studios; he claims Dubby has appeared—in one form or another—to all of them. Lang told a reporter from *The Stranger*: "Everybody. Every engineer that has worked here—every one of 'em—has come in contact with a supernatural phenomenon ..."

Those haunted happenings run the gamut of paranormal phenomena: Doors open and close by themselves. People report sudden and inexplicable chills. Ghostly voices and sounds echo without any visible source.

But it's the apparitions that have everyone talking. A few people have even captured images of what they claim to be apparitions in the studio. One of the most famous is a picture taken by the drummer for a band called Drown Mary. The drummer decided to snap a picture of the band's bassist, who was alone in the shot, playing his bass at the time. But the photo shows a filmy fog—that some say resembles the haunted spirit depicted in artist Edvard Munch's "The Scream."

Critics, though, just say it's an odd reflection, or a smudge.

But Robert Lang Studios has a way of converting skeptics. The members of the Afghan Whigs, another band that recorded at the studios, were less skeptical about the paranormal after their recording session there.

It all started when the band began to experience some weird and unexpected problems with the tape recorder. They also heard strange noises and saw lights flicker violently. Despite repeated attempts to mitigate the problems, the engineers couldn't figure out why the equipment was malfunctioning.

It shouldn't have been a major surprise for the members of the Afghan Whigs. For years, bands have talked about the equipment malfunctions, noises, and sudden drops in temperature that have accompanied recording sessions in the studios. But, unlike most bands who persevered and were usually rewarded with a brilliantly recorded album, the Afghan Whigs were willing to channel their Scooby-Doo side and investigate the creepy goings-on in the building.

Greg Dulli, the band's lead singer, decided to call in some help. His friend was a psychic medium who was used to dealing with supernatural forces. She came to the studio and began to gather her impressions of the place.

Her verdict wasn't what the increasingly fearful band members were hoping for. The building was haunted, she said. The spirit was using the electronic gear as a way to manifest itself, she told the band. Her remedy was to work with the spirit and gain his—or her—cooperation so the band could record the rest of the album in peace.

As the band waited and watched, the medium burned sage, which is supposed to help purge an area of evil supernatural forces. John Curley, who played bass for the band, told *The Stranger* that the intervention appeared to work. There were no more equipment malfunctions or weird occurrences during the rest of the session.

Since the incident took place, Curley has taken a measured, reasoned approach to the strange events at Robert Lang Studios.

"What happened there was odd, but I wouldn't go as far as to say it proves anything," said Curley. "Certainly the place has that kind of vibe, even for someone who'd consider himself a skeptic."

CHAPTER 18

THE CAVE:

Billy Bob Thornton Gets Spirited Help in His Recording Studio

It's affectionately called "the Cave."

Sure, it's dark and secluded. But, according to some of the musicians who have recorded in the Beverly Hills studio, the nickname works on a whole other level. The Cave has paranormal secrets that are just as deep and just as dark as any geological hole in the ground.

The recording studio was part of an estate with a history and reputation that only Tinseltown could dream up. It was once a speakeasy during Prohibition. Secret passages were built under the property to connect Beverly Hills with West Hollywood. It was the perfect way to smuggle booze. You can only imagine what types of characters were involved in that type of business.

Early movie magnate Cecil B. DeMille also owned a house on the property.

There is a general rule with the paranormal that the more a place is connected with history—especially history of high drama and emotion—the higher the likelihood that the spot will be haunted. Emotions just have a tendency to weld themselves to the fabric of an area, long after the people associated with that high drama have physically moved on.

The Cave's close connection to some of Hollywood's biggest names and historical events could be one reason for the ghostly activity there, according to paranormal experts and Hollywood historians.

Perhaps the most famous person to go on record about the ghosts at the Cave is—at the time of this writing—the owner of the studio: actor, director, and Academy Award–winning screenwriter Billy Bob Thornton. Thornton, who wrote and directed the 1996 film *Sling Blade* and starred in a long list of blockbusters, even subtitled his biography *A Cave Full of Ghosts*.

Thornton, who is also a musician and songwriter, told *Maxim* magazine that the recording studio on the property was an added benefit when he was house shopping, but he didn't expect a co-songwriter to come along with the premises. The actor said that when he's writing a song and, like all songwriters do, gets stuck on a line, a sudden wave of inspiration will hit him. A perfect line will hit him from nowhere, he said.

"Maybe the ghost is helping me out," he told the magazine.

But there are other signs that a ghost is on the prowl in the Cave besides the sudden and inexplicable gusts of inspiration. Strange noises and odd feelings permeate the premises.

So who or what is behind the haunting at Billy Bob's studio? Some of the best sources say it's a female spirit, but no one knows exactly who she is. She may have been a starlet, or possibly a poor lady who got caught up on the wrong side of the nefarious liquor-running mobsters who once used the property as a base of operations.

Thornton isn't so sure the ghost is a woman. He believes the source of at least some of the haunted activity is a relatively new spirit and one who is closer to his heart. Warren Zevon, singer and songwriter, recorded one of his last tunes with Billy Bob and his friends at the studio.

The song, poignantly enough, was Bob Dylan's "Knocking on Heaven's Door."

When they recorded the tune, Zevon's friends knew it was probably going to be his last. The creator of "Werewolves of London" was stricken with cancer at the time of the recording. He died in September of 2003.

Zevon, known for his quirky sense of humor, may still be playing a few tricks on his old jam-session buddy—even showing up on Thornton's records. Thornton claims you can hear evidence of supernatural intervention on one of his solo albums.

"On my last solo record, there were a couple of noises that didn't seem to come from any place we could identify," Thornton told *Maxim*.

There have been suggestions that Thornton will sell the Cave, but the impressions that the haunted studio has made will follow Thornton's future creative endeavors far into the future. The mansion, no doubt, waits to make an impression on its future owners as well.

CHAPTER 19

THE MANSION:
This Studio Gets Five Red Hot Chili Peppers for Paranormal Activity

Tucked in the neighborhood of Laurel Canyon, not too far from Hollywood—which should be renamed Hauntedwood—is a mansion that Rick Rubin, record producer extraordinaire, turned into a hit-making machine for groups like the Red Hot Chili Peppers and Audioslave. Groups that record there, though, have to pay a paranormal price for studio time. The place is extremely haunted.

Chad Smith, drummer for the Red Hot Chili Peppers, does not need to be convinced. When the band decided to record their supernaturally charged album *Blood Sugar Sex Magik* at Rubin's recording studio, Smith, unlike the rest of the band, refused to stay overnight in the posh digs. He commuted to the studio every morning on his motorcycle to avoid any run-ins with the spirits that most of the members and crew agreed inhabited the place.

Another member of the band, John Frusciante, said that he agreed with Smith that the Mansion was haunted, but he wasn't as afraid of the paranormal activity as his band mate.

"There are definitely ghosts in the house," Frusciante said. However, he described the ghosts as friendly and the experience as positive. "We have nothing but warm vibes and happiness everywhere we go in this house."

The Red Hot Chili Peppers said that they actually have photographic proof of spirit activity. A photograph taken for the artwork on the *Blood Sugar Sex Magik* album contains an orb. Look closely at the orb and you can see a face. It may be the face of the spirit that haunts the Mansion and has watched over the recording of one of rock history's most creative, inventive albums.

Rubin and the Chilis aren't the only ones who have sensed and seen a presence in the home. The property has a long paranormal history. Paranormal experts indicate that the hauntings began in the early twentieth century.

Before it was ever a famous recording studio, the property contained a run-of-the-mill mansion for Los Angeles's wealthy set. After all, there's nothing extraordinary about a mansion in L.A. According to legend, the son of a wealthy furniture store owner lived in the mansion with his parents. While little has been reported about this furniture magnate's son, it's easy to get the impression that he was a typical spoiled Los Angeles brat. One day, in a fit of rage, a fit of jealousy, or just a fit, the son pushed his lover off the balcony.

That murder victim's spirit still haunts the property.

The mansion burned down, but new owners rebuilt the current structure that stands on the grounds today. Still, a little fire didn't seem to singe the spirit's or spirits' attachment to the scenic spot. (That should give you some idea of how expensive it is to find a new place in L.A.)

The list of rock musicians who have experienced strange goings-on at the Mansion is as long as the rows of gold and platinum albums that Rubin has amassed in his career.

You would think that if you name your band Slipknot—which was the knot of choice for hanging criminals in the Wild West—then you should know a thing or two about the dead. But the band was totally unprepared for their encounter with the spirits at the Mansion. Sources say that the band witnessed a number of weird events while recording an album, but the weirdest involved drummer Joey Jordison.

Jordison said that while he was in the basement, he felt that a ghost, or some sort of presence, had walked through him. Band mate Corey Taylor took pictures of two orbs hovering near the thermostat of his room. He said that prior to this, he had noticed that something was changing the temperature settings on the thermostat.

Members from other bands said they heard and saw doors open and close by themselves and equipment operating oddly. Cedric Bixler Zavala, who performs with the Mars Volta, said he and the rest of the group especially avoided the room known as the Bell Tower because it seemed so haunted.

The range of experiences at the Mansion—from the benign to the really weird—indicates that there may be more than one presence that haunts the property. But as long as the studio churns out multiplatinum albums, bands are not going to be frightened off by a ghost—or a whole band of ghosts.

CHAPTER 20

EARNESTINE and HAZEL'S:

The Blues, the Booze, and the Boos at Memphis's Most Rockingest, Hauntedest Hotspot

Memphis is described by some rock historians as the geographic and spiritual nexus of rock and roll.

Country and western music, mined and chiseled to fine perfection in Nashville, wandered west into Memphis by the Mississippi River. Hot blues creeped east from the heart of the swamps and Deep South. The raucous rhythms of the new music pulsed through Beale Street, the city's hardscrabble, somewhat seedy section. In the mid-twentieth century, musicians like Elvis Presley and B.B. King pulled in all these influences and, like wizards, mixed a blend of blues, gospel, and country music into a magical musical potion that became rock and roll.

Without Memphis, there would be no rock and roll.

Memphis isn't just a hotbed of rock. The city also happens to be one of the hottest hotbeds of haunted activity in the United States. And just as music has an important place in nearly every aspect of Memphis's culture and history, it also plays a key role in the city's paranormal legacy.

The city's famous bars, clubs, auditoriums, and concert venues play host to a list of restless souls and angry spirits, according to the city's experts on the paranormal. Earnestine and Hazel's is one of the places in Memphis where live musicians—and, apparently, dead people, too—continue to mix it up in the city's downtown.

Michael Einspanjer is intimately familiar with the ghosts of Memphis. As leader of Memphis Paranormal Investigations, he's gone directly into the heart of the city's paranormal underbelly to bring back eyewitness accounts, pictures, and electronic voice phenomena as evidence.

The tales range from the interesting to the terrifying.

For Einspanjer, researching ghosts and spirits isn't a hobby, it's a mission, and he makes no bones about it that he has no time for amateur ghost hunters. It was that type of commitment to uncovering the truth about hauntings that brought him to Earnestine and Hazel's, located on South Main Street. The bar is considered one of the rockingest spots in Memphis. And it is also considered one of the "hauntedest spots in Memphis," as Einspanjer calls it.

Coming from Einspanjer, that means something. He has made the investigation into the haunting of Earnestine and

Hazel's a central case study in his career as a researcher of supernatural phenomena.

The researcher has said that most people familiar with the case would suggest that events in the strange history of Earnestine and Hazel's may be the cause of its paranormal activity. The first floor was once an apothecary and sundries store. Speaking of sundries, the second floor of the building served different needs. It was a brothel.

This mix of sex, booze, and hair care products may have triggered the ghostly events that people have witnessed at the juke joint over the decades, most experts theorize. However, according to Einspanjer, it wasn't too unusual for a business in that section of Memphis at the turn of the twentieth century to have a little side business going on upstairs.

The bar was later a watering hole and concert venue for some of the area's best musical acts. Wilson Pickett was rumored to have played there and done some of his best writing in the bar, creating a few of his classics in the establishment. It later even served as a backdrop for a Loretta Lynn–Jack White video.

There were more than great songs coming out of Earnestine and Hazel's. There were great ghost stories, too. The list of phenomena that people have encountered in the bar includes moans and disembodied voices. Some of this has been captured by ghost hunters using EVP equipment. Folks who have had experiences at the bar listed a few spirit suspects in the case of Earnestine and Hazel's haunting, including the ghost of a prostitute.

Einspanjer was called in for a series of investigations. During Einspanjer's investigations, he found some examples of this vocalized type of activity. He heard voices and captured some impressive EVPs. On a few occasions, he heard what sounded like footsteps walking up and down the stairs. He witnessed physical phenomena, too. Doors opened and closed by themselves during the investigations, just as other people had witnessed.

For most of us, this type of activity would be enough to send us screaming into the streets, but not for Einspanjer, who has endured a couple of really close encounters with spirits. This evidence was "neat," as Einspanjer put it, but, at least in his lengthy paranormal experience, nothing too out of the ordinary for a guy who investigates out-of-the-ordinary things all the time.

That designation changed for the investigator, however, when he wrapped up a so-so investigation at the bar and filmed some of what he considers the best proof of the paranormal in his career. In fact, he believes it may be some of the most convincing evidence of ghostly encounters ever.

He explained that the encounter happened as he made one final call to any spirits present. Usually, when Einspanjer is about to shut off the camera, he calls out and tells any spirits present that they have one final shot to make an appearance.

He no sooner uttered the words in the bar when the jukebox kicked on.

That wasn't that unusual at Earnestine and Hazel's. The jukebox, after all, is supposedly haunted, or is at least a medium that the spirits use to reveal themselves, according to the paranormal researcher.

One thing did strike Einspanjer, though. When the jukebox popped on, the lyrics were, "Can you see me? Can you see the real me?" He had to wonder whether the spirits were using the lyrics as a message. Einspanjer didn't think much more about the whole incident until he examined the footage and saw the unmistakable image of a man walking through the camera shot.

"It's definitely an African American male walking by with a white pillar candle," Einspanjer said. "The clothes are not from this era, either."

The researcher posted the video on the group's website and called film experts and people who work in television production to try to debunk the footage. So far, there hasn't been a natural explanation. Einspanjer, his own biggest debunker, did his best to re-create the scene and see if the man could have just been someone who happened to be walking by the shot. But one part seemed elusive: as the spirit walks past the window, you can see that the figure is transparent.

"You can see right through it," Einspanjer said, adding, "I tried to re-create that just about every way I could and couldn't come close to that."

Haunted jukeboxes and transparent guests aren't the only bizarre activity at the bar. Not all of the supernatural events can be seen or heard, either; they have to be felt.

At a certain point, as guests walk to the top of a set of stairs in Earnestine and Hazel's, they become overwhelmed with a sense of sadness. According to Einspanjer, this emotional connection may be drawn from the spirit of a prostitute who reportedly died in the bathroom. He's had dozens of people tell him about how they instantly became sad and desperate as they walked through the exact same spot.

Einspanjer realizes these folks may just be picking up on visual cues from each other. But he can't explain what happened when he led a first-time visitor to Earnestine and Hazel's up the haunted staircase. As this man walked up the steps, just like hundreds of other guests, he began to cry.

What made this incident different, explained Einspanjer, was that this visitor was blind. There was no way visual cues had triggered the emotional response.

For Einspanjer and dozens of other paranormal researchers, this was just one more piece of evidence that led them to conclude that Earnestine and Hazel's isn't just one of the most haunted sites in Memphis's rock and roll history, it's one of the most haunted sites in Memphis, period.

CHAPTER 21

THE CRUMP:
G.H.O.S.T.S in the C.R.U.M.P.

A visit to the Crump is a little like a trip to the past, back to a time when downtown sidewalks were packed with people looking for some fun and action on a Saturday night and when theaters were the cultural center of the city.

It was a time when rock ruled.

During that time, the iconic Crump Theatre was Columbus, Indiana's entertainment mecca, whether you wanted to watch a movie, see a play, or check out the latest rock and roll act to come to town. The Crump has reinvented itself several times over the years, but recently, the crown jewel of Columbus's downtown has received a super—and, some might say, a supernatural—makeover.

In addition to continuing its service as a cultural hub in the community, the theater is now a center for ghost hunters, paranormal researchers, and other fans of the supernatural who are looking for a good time—with a ghost. The researchers head to the Crump because it is one of the most haunted places in the city and arguably one of the most paranormally active spots in the extremely haunted Hoosier State.

Built in the 1870s as the city's opera house, the Crump hosted some of the biggest legends of rock and roll. In fact, John Mellencamp, who back then went by the snazzier name of John Cougar, said he got his real start playing at the Crump. As a testament to the Crump's influence on his career, Mellencamp—who wrote and performed a bunch of smashes, including "Jack and Diane" and "R.O.C.K. in the U.S.A"—staged a television special there. Recently, other rock acts and rap artists have added the Crump to their must-play list of concert venues.

The artists who performed at the Crump throughout its long history, as well as audience members and workers, have told and retold stories about supernatural encounters there. It's probably no surprise that a theater with great acoustics has a few vocal spirits. Strange, disembodied voices and moans echo through the halls, according to reports. Witnesses also talk about creaking and cracking floors and chairs. Maybe it's just that old buildings creak and crack without any spirit help, but witnesses say that there seems to be an intelligent force behind the noises. For instance, the creaks across the floor sound like someone is walking, and the chair cracks sound exactly like someone is sitting down or adjusting his or her position in the chair.

In addition to snippets of EVPs that ghost hunters have collected over the years, paranormal experts have gathered an exhaustive list of anomalous phenomena, including cold spots and sudden, ominous feelings that someone—or something—is watching them.

Paranormal buffs who visit the theater in order to have a supernatural experience say the building has an odd atmosphere that's a little hard to describe. It's almost like the living are the ghosts, and the spirits that haunt the place are, well, just going about their everyday routines. You can feel like the intruder in the Crump, according to some people.

Jason Baker, founder and administrator of Midwestern Researchers and Investigators of Paranormal Activity (MRIPA), has had that feeling a few times while investigating the hauntings at the Crump. The organization, which has been investigating all forms of anomalous activity since 1996, has been featured several times in the media, including the History Channel.

Baker, who is a third-generation paranormal investigator continuing a family tradition started by his late grandfather, said investigations in the Crump rarely disappoint. The group has investigated the Crump on multiple occasions, and the theater is usually so active and so interesting that they use the place to train and mentor other paranormal researchers.

Nearly every investigation—meticulously recorded and documented by Baker and his group—adds more evidence to the Crump's paranormal reputation. They have collected a veritable vault of video and voice evidence of the supernatural at work—and play—in the theater.

While the activity in most hauntings is centered in a certain section of a home or building, such as the basement or a bedroom, the hauntings at the Crump are different. Baker says the activity at the Crump doesn't seem to be confined to one area in the theater; the whole place is haunted. Groups have encountered spirits in nearly every room of every floor.

During one investigation, the group brought in a friend who is also a medium—a person who claims to be able to contact the spirit world. As she passed down through the aisles of seats, she said—on camera—that her hand was hot when she touched a certain seat. Later, while the team checked for EVPs, they picked something up just as the medium's hand touched the seat and she complained of a hot sensation in her hand.

"You can clearly hear on the recording a voice saying, 'That's my seat,'" Baker said in the interview.

Another incident wasn't captured through EVP equipment. Pretty much everyone on the investigation team heard it, though. According to Baker, the MRIPA members were starting to set up when they heard a calliope play. There was no mistaking the sound of this distinct musical instrument. Baker ran to the recorder and turned it on, but the equipment inexplicably didn't work. The carnival-sounding music faded as abruptly as it started. After trying to debunk the incident, the team agreed that it was just another example of the Crump haunting.

Most of the group members, including Baker, believe that the haunting at the Crump is interactive and friendly. That's another reason they use the theater to conduct investigations with new members and mentor investigators from other teams. The risk of having an encounter with any seriously negative paranormal energy is low at the Crump.

Baker speculates that the theater has somehow picked up all of the positive energies drawn from the audience members and performers during its storied past and now reflects that energy back into the present.

"Well, think about it. You have all these people who are going out to see a show and are ready to hit the town and then you have performers excited about putting on a show for five or six thousand people," Baker said. "You can just imagine the type of energy that's created over the years."

CHAPTER 22

FIRST AVENUE:
Paranormal Reign

Prince and the Revolution helped make the First Avenue nightclub world famous.

But long before Prince, the club was famous among fans of the paranormal. First Avenue, one of the premier spots for live music and dance music in Minneapolis, Minnesota, has a patron—or maybe a whole group of patrons—who seem to ignore the bartender's request for last call.

This customer never goes home.

Performers, their crews, music lovers, and bar hoppers continue to file reports of the strange goings-on at First Avenue, which once served as one of the Twin Cities' Greyhound bus stations. The club's unique art-deco exterior and extensive list of celebrities who have performed there have made it an iconic stretch of real estate in the city. Everyone knows about First Avenue. Prince played there, of course, and even as his career exploded, he continued to use the club as a base of operations, allowing him to explore new material on the First Avenue stage. Several scenes from Prince's 1984 movie *Purple Rain* were filmed there. You could get funky at First Avenue on some nights—and you could get punky on others. The club played a prominent role in Minneapolis's punk rock movement, showcasing bands such as Hüsker Dü and the Replacements.

While the history of First Avenue has been permanently etched into the annals of rock and roll history, its ghostly history is a little harder to pin down. Many people who are familiar with the haunting are often conflicted about whose ghost is the cause of the strange activity going on in the club.

One thing is for certain: the haunting seems to have more to do with a lady in a green jacket than with a girl in a raspberry beret. You can trace the origin of the haunting back to the 1970s. That's when the stories began to circulate that a female ghost was haunting the building.

Although the details vary, there seem to be two spectral themes. In one version, people say they see an apparition of a thin woman. People guess that the apparition is the ghost of a woman who died of a drug overdose when the building was used as a bus station. In another version, a woman who hanged herself in the club's ladies' room continues to haunt the property.

According to paranormal researchers, both stories sound plausible. Bus stations can certainly draw their share of lost souls—the homeless, the desperate, etc. Those lost souls—in the earthly sense—are often prime suspects for hauntings when they leave this mortal coil. Suicide victims are also prime suspects in cases like this.

When witnesses describe the apparition, it actually could fit either theory, but it tends to lend more credence to the theory that the apparition is the ghost of a suicide victim. Witnesses have described a blonde woman dressed in a green jacket who appears—and then vanishes inexplicably.

Like so many other aspects of this haunting, it's hard to classify this supernatural activity. The ghost interacts with people, according to some accounts. That makes it an intelligent haunting. But the spirit often seems oblivious to the living while it single-mindedly goes about its mysterious business. Researchers would say that is a sign of a residual haunting.

It's easy to dismiss the accounts of a bunch of slightly tipsy club goers, but sober and rational members of the staff have also reported the ghost, who has been seen so many times by so many employees that she's been nicknamed "the Lady in Green."

One guest at the club reported that she had a close encounter with the Lady in Green, who seemed to want to communicate with her. She said that she went to the ladies' room in the club and saw a blonde woman wearing a green jacket. The woman in the green jacket was animated, struggling desperately to tell the witness something. She believes the Lady in Green was showing her how she died.

Other extremely unlucky patrons have gotten a much ruder introduction to the Lady in Green. According to some accounts, customers will enter the bathroom, open the stall door, and see a woman hanging from the ceiling, a grisly re-creation of the suicide that started the haunting, believers say.

Other witnesses say the ghost isn't always despairing over her sad fate or reenacting her final tragic moments; sometimes she hits the dance floor. People have sworn that as they were looking across the dance floor full of people pulsating to the music, they noticed a striking blonde woman. She seems to be having a great time. But as their eyes drift down to the floor, they notice something shocking: she doesn't have any legs. The apparition appears from the waist up—and her fellow dancers grind on, oblivious.

The rumors of hauntings have been so persistent at the club over the years that at least one paranormal research team has been called in to investigate. The team investigated the club several times, and while the group can't say officially that the place is haunted—it requires a lot of evidence for that—one of the group's founders said that there seem to be indications of supernatural activity in the club.

Besides its role as a bus stop, the building was also home to a slaughterhouse and a school. Since the building has such a long and varied history, researchers say it's tricky to pinpoint the origin of the spooky activity.

Inside, the building has a meandering and multilayered structure, which can hamper gathering EVPs and, generally speaking, makes paranormal investigations a little more challenging. However, ghost hunters have recorded a number of EVPs, including one in the bathroom that is center stage for several ghost stories at the club.

According to one research team, a shadow flitted by, and another researcher said that his shirt was tugged. He saw the fabric of the shirt move away from his body and hover briefly.

The building has several basements. In one, a researcher said that he found a chair, sat down, and leaned back. Whether the chair was unstable or some spirit was playing a prank on the investigator is anybody's guess, but as he leaned back, the chair buckled a little and gave way, causing him to yell out, "Whoa!" The team thought they heard an odd noise as the man grappled with the chair. Later, when they listened to the recording, they heard a distinct giggle.

In a marriage of science and spirituality, paranormal research teams often call in psychic mediums to verify the evidence gathered through the researchers' scientific equipment, such as recorders, electromagnetic field detectors, and cameras. Psychic mediums apparently have picked up on the activity in the club. In some cases, the evidence gathered by the equipment and the mediums appears to corroborate. One investigator claimed that during an investigation, an infrared camera caught a strange object flitting across the camera. As soon as the object appeared on camera, the medium who was helping the team immediately said she was receiving an impression. Then, as the object floated by her, the psychic's eyes traced the exact path as the object—which could only be seen in the infrared spectrum—as it flew by. In the pitch-dark conditions in the club during the investigation, there was no way that the medium could have followed the object visually, according to the researcher.

Investigators won't yet conclude that there is a definite haunting at the club, nor will they conclude that the lady in green is an actual ghost who walks the halls and parties on the dance floor. After conducting dozens of investigations, credible paranormal research teams have raised the bar pretty high on those types of determinations. According to investigators, while the evidence that has been collected so far is tantalizing, more work is needed.

CHAPTER 23

CINCINNATI'S MUSIC HALL:

Supernatural Power to Soothe the Savage Breast

They say that history speaks. At Cincinnati's Music Hall, it sings.

Rock legends like Bob Dylan have performed here. But the long history of the city's regal-looking music hall, which is perched at the corner of 14th at Elm, includes famous performers from a long stretch of musical eras, from John Philip Sousa to Igor Stravinsky and from Leonard Bernstein to Miles Davis.

They all made their mark here.

But others have made their mark, too—and they don't seem to want to stop. Restless spirits haunt Music Hall, according to performers, concert goers, and dozens of workers at the hall. Paranormal researchers and ghost hunters from around the country have classified some of the reports of run-ins at Music Hall as among the best proof that the paranormal exists.

Many owners of paranormal properties try to bury—pun completely intended—the supernatural evidence because they are afraid of scaring away guests and potential customers. Fortunately for us, Music Hall's preservation society has kept meticulous records of not just the history of the concert hall but also of the hauntings and strange goings-on that have happened there. The society has invited paranormal research teams to investigate the property and encourages people to explore the paranormal side of the hall during ghost tours. The evidence gathered by these research teams and the testimony passed to the society from regular theater patrons and employees have built a pretty convincing case that the concert hall is haunted.

It's important to point out that folks who have witnessed the paranormal in the concert hall include some of the most credible people on the payroll. One music director said that he had a few encounters with the supernatural while toiling away during nights and early mornings on programs and arrangements. Erich Kunzel, the late Cincinnati Pops music director, had thought the spirits were friendly and had challenged skeptics.

"They are definitely in this building, some sort of spirits," Kunzel reported on the music hall society's website. "If anyone thinks I'm nuts, come here at 3:00 in the morning or 4:00 in the morning."

The top rung of the corporate ladder isn't immune to the hauntings, either.

Patricia Beggs, CEO and general director of the Cincinnati Opera, has felt another presence in the building, even when she was alone working at night. She has also reported a story of one of the music hall's employees bringing his son along to work. As his father worked, the son was enjoying himself on his visit, playing on the world-famous stage.

Suddenly, the boy turned to his dad and asked, "Who's that man in the box?" The boy indicated that there was someone in one of the boxes where the music director typically sat during a performance. The father looked. There was no one there. At least he didn't see anyone. He calmly explained to his three-year-old that there was no man in the box. But his son insisted.

"Yes, there is," the boy said emphatically. "He's waving at me."

By now, everyone was totally creeped out, and the artists and crew made a hasty retreat from the music hall for the evening.

Perhaps one of the most dramatic and convincing cases of spirit activity in Music Hall is the detailed account by John Engst, a night watchman at the music hall in 1987. Engst was so deeply moved by the event that he wrote down his story and allowed it to be kept for permanent history.

Engst was escorting a group of ladies out of the building after a party that was held to celebrate that night's successful performance. The group entered the elevator and rode it down toward the lobby. While it didn't mean much to Engst at the time, the women asked the night watchman if he could hear music. He said he didn't hear any. But the ladies were insistent: they could hear music.

Once they exited the elevator, the women continued to claim that they could hear music. Engst strained and listened, and then he could hear music. Not only could he hear it, but he could make out the tune. It was "Let Me Call You Sweetheart." He wrote in his account that the tune "wasn't loud," but that it was "beautiful and voluminous." The women asked Engst to go back up in the elevator and investigate. At first he was hesitant, but then he agreed.

Now, that's dedication.

He went back into the elevator to find the source of the music—and the tune became stronger and clearer. As soon as the elevator stopped and Engst stepped onto the floor, the music abruptly stopped. The hall became completely, utterly silent, like a shroud had softly descended, separating him from the source of this spectral orchestra. It's important to note that the concert hall did not subscribe to a Muzak service to pipe in tunes to the elevator.

The confused night watchman never found the source of the haunting elevator music. Even weeks later, his body would tingle each time he approached the elevator. Engst said the encounter—while scary at the time—left him less worried about death and much more of a believer in the afterlife.

Engst wasn't the only one who took a ride on the wild side in the music hall's elevator. Other witnesses have stepped forward and told concert hall officials that they didn't just hear music, they heard voices while riding on the elevator.

It's one thing to have a visit from a ghost on an elevator ride, or one playing a tune for you, but it's quite another to have a ghost touch you, as one box office worker at Music Hall would be certain to tell you.

According to the account, the employee was at the box office window when he heard the ding of the buzzer, indicating there was a customer at the window. Except he was at the window—and there was no one there.

The buzzer kept going off. Incessantly.

But the worker could clearly see that the area in front of the window was empty.

The buzzing continued with such persistence that the man finally left the box office and went outside to look around. He figured the buzzer was broken, or perhaps there was an electrical problem. However, after a quick inspection he saw no initial signs of any mechanical problem.

Once he reentered the box office, right on cue, the buzzing started all over again. He went back outside to see if he could find the source of the problem. The odd behavior of the buzzer had thoroughly unnerved the worker. He noted that rather than having a random buzzing pattern that would indicate that there was some sort of electronic glitch causing the activity, the buzzing had a rhythmic persistence that sounded exactly like a human being was pressing the button to get his attention.

But that was just the beginning. The evening was going to change from the just plain weird to completely life changing for the box office worker.

At a certain point during the night, the man said he felt a tug at his elbow. He looked down and saw, as plain as day, a young boy dressed in short pants and a cap—the fashion of a bygone era—tugging at him.

The worker was shocked. The spirit then disappeared as fast as he had appeared.

Who was the young spirit?

Nobody at the music hall has a clue, and it's just one more piece in the puzzle about why Music Hall is one of the most haunted spots in the city. Some people say that the story about the ghost of the little boy is proof that the hall is haunted by spirits of past audience members. They had such a good time at the concerts and shows at the hall that they just keep coming back—over and over and over.

That's one of the favorite and more benign theories.

Another theory points to the music hall's unique geographic location. The building was erected near the site where an insane asylum and an orphanage once stood. Rumor has it that the bodies of many homeless, insane, and other of the city's lost souls were buried on the land.

Ask anyone in the paranormal research field and they will tell you that one way to stir up some spirits is to disturb a few graves. Another way is to build near the scene of trauma and drama—like an insane asylum.

Both of these were the case with Music Hall. Experts in the paranormal suggest that's why the music hall has ghosts. Lots of ghosts.

SECTION III

PREMONITIONS, SIGNS, AND OMENS OF ROCK AND ROLL

The future appears walled off from us. At best, we can try to guess at what might happen to us in the future. We call these guesses hopes, fears, worries, and dreams. But there are those who believe that the future is accessible to all of us, right here and right now.

We just need to know where to look—and, especially, how to look. After all, you cannot part the clouds of the misty future by following a written set of bold-print directions or watching a how-to video on prognostication.

The future is funny about being probed. It may decide to reveal itself, but it won't do so easily. Sometimes the future symbolically reveals itself through strange signs that we call omens or synchronicities. The veil of the future must be carefully lifted and then it must be deciphered.

History is full of people who use a variety of techniques and tactics to predict the future—people we usually refer to as fortunetellers, soothsayers, or prophets. For our primitive ancestors, the skies at night were alight with the signs and symbols of the future. The movements of planets and stars could tell hunters where they could find game, or what dangers might lurk around the corner, according to those early astrologers. Before 1-800 fortunetellers were just a phone call away, Greeks marched to the Oracle at Delphi to have their fortune discerned, often through riddles or vague sayings. The ancient Chinese tossed runes and coins to predict the future, while others scoured animal entrails—yuck—and examined the sky for a hint of things to come.

Rock history, in particular, is full of people who don't need runes or entrails to tell the future. The future reveals itself through dreams, sudden flashes of insight, or just deep-down feelings that won't seem to go away.

Signs and omens, as well as premonitions, are a part of rock and roll's occult lore, too. While premonitions are typically strong impressions or dreams that foretell the future, signs and omens are external events that may foretell the future.

Not all premonitions or signs are ominous. There can be fortuitous signs. Rock history is filled with stories of hungry musicians who have had dreams or visions of success that followed them into the real world. Strange events may point the way for would-be rock stars to climb to the summit of the charts.

But there are other signs that have predicted disaster for rock and rollers. Rock historians have interpreted certain events in the careers of famous rock musicians—like tragic coin tosses, or sudden visions in the desert—as omens of plane crashes and other untimely deaths.

We'll take a look at rock and roll signs, omens, and premonitions—both good and bad—in our next section.

CHAPTER 24

ELVIS PRESLEY:
The King of Destiny

Nobody would have predicted that the little ragamuffin born in Tupelo, Mississippi, on January 8, 1935, would even become successful, let alone turn into the central icon in rock's pantheon of gods and goddesses. Heck, they would have been hard-pressed to believe that the forces of destiny would have led Elvis any further than the careers of truck drivers and blues musicians he seemed so keen to emulate as a teen.

He had a couple strikes against him. First, Elvis Aron Presley, the once and future King of Rock and Roll, was poor. In a very poor community, the Presleys were among the poorest.

Second, his family was a little sketchy. Elvis's dad, Vernon, was a laborer who skirted the law with some of his money-making schemes to lift his family out of poverty. There were allegations that he was a moonshiner, and he was busted for trying to alter a check to get more money from his employer.

Most people say the shame of that event pushed the family to move to Memphis.

No one would have guessed that Vernon's son would have a future any brighter than his father's. But Gladys, Elvis's mother, had much higher expectations for her boy. She—and maybe she alone—sensed that he was going to be special.

Elvis must have picked up some of this confidence in his own destiny. He once said, "I never believed that anything was a coincidence. There's a reason for everything that happens."

Gladys believed that one of the family's earliest tragedies was a key to his supernatural powers. Elvis had an older twin brother, Jesse Garon, born thirty-five minutes before Elvis. Jesse, though, was stillborn. Even though he died, Jesse's spirit followed Elvis, or at least that's what his mom believed. It was a belief she instilled in her son. Gladys said that Elvis could consider Jesse as his guardian angel, a guiding spirit that would lead him to his destiny.

Gladys, who was steeped in the charismatic religious beliefs of the South, told Elvis that he actually had the spiritual power of two people and that this special power would lead him to fame and fortune. Friends and neighbors of the Presley family noticed that Elvis would sometimes talk to himself. But he wasn't talking to himself. He was talking to Jesse, his twin brother and guardian angel.

Even later in life, Elvis would speak about Jesse not as a deceased brother, but as a real, palpable presence. Larry Geller, Elvis's hairdresser and spiritual confidant, said that Elvis never came to terms with Jesse's death. When he talked with Elvis about his brother, the conversations typically made Elvis cry.

Right before his death, Elvis had a dream about his twin that Geller guessed was a premonition of the star's own pending death. In the dream, Elvis said he was performing and looked across the stage and saw his twin, who looked and dressed just like Elvis. There was one thing that was different about the two brothers, Elvis said. Jesse had a better voice! The two began to perform together, much to the delight of Elvis's dream audience.

People who analyze dreams to discover what the future holds would say that Elvis had a reintegration dream. He and his twin were rejoining—at least symbolically. Elvis, too, speculated that maybe the dream was a premonition. He was getting ready to join his brother in heaven.

It wasn't the only time that Elvis sensed his end was near.

Elvis had a nuanced—but somewhat typical for the rural South at the time—view of spirituality and the afterlife. In some areas of the South, Christianity and folk religions exist harmoniously, even though some elements are contradictory. Snake handlers and blue laws, Pentecostal healing services and folk medicine spells all are part of the rich spiritual tapestry that Elvis was likely exposed to as he grew up.

As an adult, his experimentation with spiritual beliefs continued and, in fact, expanded. Not wanting to miss out on going to heaven on a technicality, Elvis tested just about every form of spirituality, from Judaism to Buddhism. But he always stayed close to his unique Southern-accented Christian roots. He could be part rock and roller and part biblical prophet, often at the same time.

For example, during a trip to Hollywood, Geller said, Elvis suddenly became agitated and pulled over the van he was driving. None of the other passengers knew what was happening. As he exited the car, Elvis exclaimed that he saw an image of Joseph Stalin, the one-time Soviet leader, in the clouds.

The image of Stalin suddenly turned into the face of Jesus Christ.

The *San Francisco Chronicle* reported that Geller said that Elvis, who proceeded to drag his hairdresser into the desert to share the vision, felt it was a revelation. He ranted to Geller, saying, "He smiled at me and every fiber of my being felt it. For the first time in my life, God and Christ are a living reality." Or was it a premonition? Maybe Elvis had just gotten a preview of meeting his maker.

During another conversation with Geller, Elvis offered an eerie prediction of his eventual end. He told Geller, "I know my fans think I'm fat, but I'm going to look good in a coffin."

Geller said he had no doubt that Elvis knew his end was near.

"Elvis had a premonition," Geller said in a story on Go Elvis.com. "He knew."

More premonitions followed. In Las Vegas, shortly before his death, Elvis asked televangelist Rex Humbard to pray with him in his dressing room at a hotel before a show around the Christmas holiday in 1976. Elvis was a fan of Humbard's televised services.

Humbard said Elvis spoke to him and praised his religious program. As he spoke to the pastor, Elvis appeared to slip into a trance. He summoned Humbard and several others into another room. For the next half hour or so, the preacher said the King of Rock and Roll was moved by the Spirit. He quoted scripture and made a prediction.

"Christ is coming soon, isn't he?" Elvis asked Humbard, who agreed, according to the preacher's biography, as well as other interviews.

Humbard said the sense of urgency in the singer's voice made him think that something much deeper was troubling Elvis.

"I think it was a premonition or something. He was reaching for something spiritual and I think he found some of what he was looking for," Humbard told the Associated Press.

In just a few short months, Humbard would see Elvis one last time. He would preach at Elvis's funeral.

CHAPTER 25

THE BEATLES:
The Future Loves You, Yeah, Yeah, Yeah

Back in the early 1960s, if someone asked you to look at a globe and place a pin in the spot where you most expected the next great rock and roll trend to start, you might pick New York City.

Or maybe Los Angeles.

Maybe even London.

How about Austin?

But the last place that pin would land would be Liverpool, the rough and tough, down and dirty seaport in England. Few people thought much of the roughneck city and even fewer had anything positive to say about the music scene there. Real musicians were from London.

Only a few lads from Liverpool, who weren't bad with guitars and drums, and a couple of their fans had any idea that they were bound to be not just rock stars, but an absolute rock phenomenon. Why were they so sure? They knew it, supposedly, because the group had seen the future.

Before taking the music world by storm, the Beatles—John Lennon, Paul McCartney, George Harrison, and Ringo Starr—were a bunch of streetwise Liverpudlians who dug American rock and roll. They weren't known as exceptional songwriters, or even decent musicians, for that matter. The only lucky thing about being born in Liverpool was that living in the port town meant the future Beatles could find American rock records, which were brought across the pond by sailors, before anyone else did.

Paul and John formed the core of the band. George joined later. Ringo wouldn't arrive until shortly before the band made its meteoric rise from a great local band to international musical trendsetters.

During those early days, the band barely eked out an existence, playing at tiny coffeehouses and the dank, dirty bars of Liverpool. They were lucky—that term is used loosely—enough to travel to Hamburg, Germany, to play in a few rowdy beer halls.

They weren't welcomed there, either. Most Liverpool bands that were doing well in Hamburg begged the concert promoters not to invite the "bum band," the Beatles, to the city. They claimed that the Beatles' lousy musicianship and totally absent professionalism would ruin the budding music scene in the city. No Liverpool band would be allowed back in the city if the Beatles came in and stunk up the scene.

The band also weathered several tragedies and personnel changes. Their bassist, Stu Sutcliffe, quit the band and later died of a brain hemorrhage. Pete Best, the Beatles' first drummer and arguably the most popular band member in those early days, was sacked, causing a near riot.

But they kept at it. They kept performing. They kept writing. They kept dreaming.

What kept them going?

It may have been a premonition, a dream that they would be stars, that kept them going during those hard times. At least that's what Paul McCartney recently suggested.

It wasn't that McCartney had a dream that he and his other band mates would be stars. He didn't see the album covers or the throngs of adoring fans that lined the streets and airport terminals when the Beatles visited their town. Anyone can have those dreams.

The dream McCartney had was more of a symbolic vision, one that he interpreted as a sign to keep going, even during the bleakest days. According to McCartney, one night he dreamed that he was digging with his hands in a garden. It was actually a recurring dream. He had dreamt several times of digging in his garden, although he never found anything, except junk. This time, though, as he dug, he discovered a gold coin.

Then another.

And another.

McCartney later speculated that "life gives you minor premonitions. You don't think of them as premonitions until the dream comes true ..." The gold coin dream has an even stranger twist. John Lennon reportedly had a nearly identical dream. Lennon, too, found treasure in his dream.

Over the next decade or so, Lennon and McCartney would find more gold—and platinum. They became the most successful songwriting duo ever, churning out hit song after hit song.

Even when the Lennon-McCartney songwriting partnership broke up and they went solo, they continued to find gold records as easily as some of us might pluck a stone from the garden.

Number 9 Dreams

If some premonitions helped guide the Beatles to stardom, other signs were portents of tragedy for the Fab Four, or at least for one of the members of the band.

Lennon appeared to be obsessed—some might say haunted—by the number 9. He was born on October 9, 1940. Brian Epstein, the manager of the Beatles, discovered the band on November 9. The Beatles debuted in the United States on the *Ed Sullivan Show* on February 9. Lennon also met his soulmate, Yoko Ono, on November 9. When Yoko and John had a child, Sean, he was born on October 9 as well.

That number hovered around Lennon's artistic life. One of the first songs he and McCartney wrote was called "The One After 909." He had another hit with "Revolution 9." A more experimental tune, called "#9 Dream," was on his fifth solo studio album and peaked at number 9 on the charts.

Maybe this was all coincidence, but believers in signs and numerology say that numbers can foreshadow coming events. Numbers are destiny. Lennon, for one, believed in numerology and always believed 9 was his lucky number. He didn't find the number ominous. However, the number 9 reappeared at a few more devastating times in Lennon's life in decidedly unlucky ways.

The rock and roll legend was gunned down by Mark David Chapman and rushed to Roosevelt Hospital on 9th Avenue, where he would finally die from the gunshot wounds. "Mark

David" and "Roosevelt" both have 9 letters, by the way. Fans were stunned to hear that Lennon was murdered on December 8, 1980.

But wait a minute. December 8th? Does that mean the number 9 omen failed?

Not so fast.

When those shots rang out in New York City and people in Lennon's hometown of Liverpool, England, awoke to hear about the tragedy, it wasn't December 8.

It was December 9.

The Seer and the Beatle

John Lennon was no stranger to tragedy. It stalked him.

His mother, Julia, died in a horrific car-pedestrian accident when Lennon was just a teenager. The event sent the young Lennon into a psychological tailspin. Full of sorrow and rage, Lennon quickly sought relief in alcohol, which nearly led to the scuttling of his new band that would later be known as the Beatles.

Later, as the band began to take shape, Stu Sutcliffe, Lennon's best friend and band mate, suffered a brain aneurysm and died. He was only twenty-one years old. Brian Epstein, the Beatles' manager, died as a result of an overdose once the band hit its pinnacle. Lennon's wife, Yoko, miscarried as the couple desperately tried to have a child. These tragedies showed that death seemed to touch—but never claim—Lennon, whose own life, in many respects, was a charmed one of fame and fortune.

But one American psychic received a strong impression that this was about to change for Lennon—and he received this vision live on radio. Though he never said Lennon's name, psychic

Alex Tanous told interviewer Lee Speigel of the NBC radio show *Unexplained Phenomena* that a famous rock star would die in an unexpected way. Tanous said the death would send shock waves through not just the American consciousness but the global consciousness. It would be a profound event.

He added that the rock star would live in America, but would not be American. Like many premonitions, Tanous's prediction did not include a name or exact date of death, but the seer allegedly wrote a list containing the names of rock stars who could be the focus of the prediction.

The interview was conducted on September 5, 1980, at the American Society for Psychical Research located on Seventy-third Street in New York City. As the television crew interviewed Tanous in his office, he could probably see one of the crown jewels of the New York City skyline, the Dakota building. John and Yoko were living in the building at the time. It would be near that building—a little over three months later—that Mark David Chapman would wait for Lennon to come home and gun him down.

Tanous's prophetic powers were uncannily on target. Lennon was living in the United States, but, of course, was born in England. The announcement of his death would ripple across not just the United States, but the world.

And the list of possible victims that Tanous made? The name John Lennon reportedly appeared right at the top.

CHAPTER 26

JOE MEEK:

The Producer and Premature Prognosticator

The name Robert George "Joe" Meek may not be as recognizable as Les Paul or Phil Spector or George Martin, but at one time, the madcap rock and roll producer was in the same league with these famous producers and musical innovators.

There are some rock historians who think he still belongs in the pantheon of all-time greatest musical producers. He has the resumé. Meek was an electronic genius with a knack for creating pop hits. How he did it, though, is a bit of a mystery. The English record producer and songwriter wasn't a musician. There are even reports that he was tone deaf. But he had a gift for choosing and collaborating with other musicians who could turn his ideas into melodies and harmonies.

Those musical collaborations led to a string of hits in England and around the world. Meek may have even laid the foundation for the British Invasion in the early 1960s when one of his hits, "Telstar," recorded by the Tornados, became the first record by an English band to ever hit number one on the American charts.

Meek was constantly experimenting with new ideas and new technologies. People said the producer was ahead of his time.

They had no idea.

Meek wasn't just obsessed with music, he was also deeply attracted to the occult. His pioneering work in electronics and radio and television technology was just a fraction of Meek's effort to reach out and touch "the other side." Meek put recording devices in graveyards to see if he could record messages from the dead. Once, he heard cats meowing and was convinced that they were spirits of the dead who were speaking and asking for help.

He didn't just rely on feline mediums to speak for the dead, he went to seances and tarot card readings where real, live human mediums provided him with important information about the future. When Meek attended one of those tarot card readings in 1958, he became convinced that he had received information that foretold the death of Buddy Holly, one of his favorite rock and roll stars.

Reportedly, the message was as simple as it was scary: "February 3rd, Buddy Holly dies."

Holly, it just so happened, was on tour in England when this message came through the astral telegraph wires to Meek. The producer tried desperately to contact Holly, but he couldn't reach him. Time was running out. The producer became more desperate and more unhinged.

He eventually contacted Holly about the grim deadline. Holly thanked Meek for the information, but, let's face it,

Meek was known as a bit of an oddball. How seriously Holly took the strange man's prediction is not known, but because February 3, 1958, came and went, Holly probably laughed off Meek's premonition.

But spirits often don't have time for long messages and, if you notice, the premonition never specified the year of Buddy Holly's death. That point was not made until a year later, on February 3, 1959, when Holly, along with his tour's accompanying acts, crashed into a cornfield in Iowa, killing all on board.

The message came a year too early.

Meek, like many others connected to Holly's career, met a horrible fate. Some readers may say he should be added to the list of Holly curse victims that we'll review a little later in the book.

Friends and family members said that the already strange Meek slipped deeper and deeper into bouts of depression and paranoia. He was intensely pained when a composer filed a lawsuit against him, claiming that Meek had stolen the melody of his most popular hit, "Telstar." The stream of royalties from the song was cut off to a trickle while the courts deliberated the case.

It may have been just one too many straws for Meek's already fragile back to carry. Police say that Meek snapped and killed his landlady, shooting her with a shotgun. Then he killed himself.

It was a sad, horrific end to a genius who once had so much promise. His talent for producing hit songs and his mastery at electronic innovation were gone. So was his gift of prophecy, apparently.

Just a few days after the murder-suicide, the court ruled that Meek did not steal the "Telstar" melody. The royalties would have been his once again.

There was one more twist to the Buddy Holly premonition. Meek, the mad musical scientist, was not the only person who had a bad feeling about Holly's tour.

Holly's new bride, Maria Elena, also had premonitions that something bad was going to happen to her husband. A series of violent, weirdly prophetic dreams disturbed her sleep right before the tour. In one, she was standing in a field when she saw a fireball streak toward the ground. The resulting explosion was deafening. Coincidentally—or perhaps not—Ritchie Valens, who accompanied Holly on that fateful air flight, also had visions of violent plane crashes years before that doomed tour.

Maria Elena woke up, distraught at the violent dream's imagery. When she told Holly the dream, he said he had had his own strange dream. In it, Holly, his own brother, and his wife were in an airplane. His brother convinced Holly to leave Maria Elena on a building while they continued on their flight.

Holly told his wife that he felt guilty for leaving her behind. He convinced Maria Elena, who was in the early stages of pregnancy and suffering from morning sickness, to stay behind during the Winter Dance Party tour.

Maria Elena's dream and Meek's message from the other world arrived too late—or perhaps with not enough force—to change Holly's destiny and save the singer and his tour mates from the tragic plane crash that, for fans around the world, was a pivotal moment that forever altered the course of pop music history.

CHAPTER 27

JOHNNY HORTON:

The Sleeping Prophet and The Rockabilly Prophet

Johnny Horton found his niche in the music scene just as country music was diverging from rock and roll. That fracture made a little musical sweet spot called rockabilly. Elvis was the first artist to sculpt out that little crevice and then turn it into the gaping chasm of rock and roll music, arguably the most popular artform of the twentieth century.

Horton, who is now a member of the Rockabilly Hall of Fame, didn't follow Elvis. He seemed content to scratch out his own niche within that niche: a little bit country, a little bit rock and roll, and a little bit folk. He didn't want to alienate either audience and ended up topping both the rock and country charts.

The singer soon became known for his storytelling ability, mastering a genre of pop that's often referred to as a "saga song." Perhaps his most popular tune was "The Battle of New

Orleans," which won a Grammy for Best Country and Western Recording back in 1960. He had another big hit with "North to Alaska."

But it's no wonder that Johnny Horton, the rockabilly artist born in Los Angeles and raised in Rusk, Texas, turned saga songs into a complete craze. He had a strange little saga of his own awaiting him.

Horton's first brush with premonitions came early in his career. The singer was a regular on some of the big tours of his time, like the Louisiana Hayride. While on those tours, he befriended many of the country and western greats, like Johnny Cash and the legend of all legends, Hank Williams.

Williams was drifting toward the downward slide of a great musical career that would define country and western music. Drinking and drugs had sapped a lot from the one-time biggest star in country music. The famous drifting cowboy had a little bit of a marriage problem, too. He had no problem getting married; it was the staying married part that Hank struggled with. He married his second wife, Billie Jean Jones, in 1952. It would also be his last marriage, not because Williams found the right woman, but because he died a few months later. Horton met Billie Jean and Williams backstage at a show. Legend has it that, mysteriously, Williams predicted that one day Horton and Billie Jean would be married.

Most blamed the strange prophecy on the copious quantity of alcohol Williams tossed back before the show, but Horton, who had an interest in the supernatural, may have wondered if there wasn't something to the weird wedding announcement. A few months after the strange prediction, Williams was dead. After an extended bender, Williams died while riding in the back of an automobile traveling to a concert in West Virginia. For a guy whose nom de plume was

"Luke the Drifter," it was a highly appropriate way to shuffle off the mortal coil. No one really knows when and where Williams died. When his driver pulled over for gas, he noticed that Williams wasn't breathing.

The rest is country music history.

Well, not quite.

A part of the Williams legacy remained. His prophecy that his wife and Horton would one day marry eventually did come true. Not too long after Williams's death, Billie Jean and the saga-singing rockabilly crooner turned the prophecy into fact. They married, just like Williams said they would.

It wasn't the only premonition to affect Horton's life. In fact, the next premonition, some believe, ended his life.

Horton became interested in the works of the "sleeping prophet," Edgar Cayce. Cayce, a good ol' boy from Kentucky, could enter a trance and access information on healings and make predictions about the future. Experts in the paranormal might refer to this as accessing the Akashic Records, a psychic space where everything that ever was—or will be—exists. Cayce later called the results of these trance sessions "readings." The sleeping prophet entered his own eternal slumber in 1945, but not after amassing thousands of hours of predictions and insights into the workings of the universe, the history of the earth, and possible keys to health.

Horton, who was a Cayce devotee, believed that this material was gospel.

While Cayce predicted things like the start of World War II and the discovery of certain strange rock formations in the Bermuda Triangle, Horton was haunted by a prophecy of his own. Friends and family said that the singer had developed a strange phobia. He became nearly obsessed with the idea that his death would be caused by a drunk.

After a performance in Texas, Horton became even more unhinged due to his fear of drinkers. He was afraid a drunk in the bar was going to kill him. The fear was so great, he didn't want to leave his dressing room. His friends and handlers had to cajole him into going on with the show. Thankfully, nothing strange happened during the show. No drunken lunatic took a shot at Horton. No boozehound interrupted the show. No drunk threatened him with a knife.

Maybe Horton felt a sense of relief. But that's the funny thing about premonitions. When you think you're in the clear and when you're confident there's nothing to fear, that is precisely the time you should start to worry.

After the show, Horton and a few of the members of his entourage jumped in a car and headed back to Shreveport, a bit over two hundred miles away. As they crossed the bridge near Milano, Texas, Horton and his crew saw a truck approach from the other side of the bridge. It began to swerve erratically, smacking first into one side of the bridge and then ricocheting into the other side. The truck then barreled straight toward Horton's vehicle. With no way to take evasive action on the bridge, there was nothing left to do but absorb the impact of the truck.

The vehicles collided.

When the rescue crews arrived at the scene of the mangled mess of metal, they saw that Horton was severely injured. He died en route to the hospital. Police didn't have to wonder why the truck lost control on the bridge. The nineteen-year-old driver was drunk.

The saga singer's weird phobia and his dire prophecy, sadly, came true.

CHAPTER 28

PATTI SMITH:
Casting the Stones

Before Patti Smith became the crown poetess of rock and roll, the high priestess of punk, and an enigmatic rock star in her own right, she was just a teenage girl with a crush on the Rolling Stones.

Even before the Stones were big in America, Smith, as precocious and as ahead of her times as ever, had already discovered the English blues-based band. She listened to their music constantly. The band would be the first major musical influence on her career, a career that most critics agree was a pioneering one for females in rock and roll. A co-writer of "Because the Night" with Bruce Springsteen, Smith recorded spoken-word poetry and became as recognized for her lyrical mastery as for her brutally stripped-down and stark music.

In 1964, she heard that the Stones were scheduled to play at a nearby high school along with the American group Patti LaBelle and the Bluebelles. Smith rushed to get tickets and snagged a front row seat. Smith and hundreds of other girls listened politely as LaBelle played.

But Smith said the mood shifted as soon as the Rolling Stones took the stage. Although the Stones weren't as famous as the advance guard of the British invasion—the Beatles—the band was quickly gaining a reputation for their charismatic and energetic blues-anchored performances.

The band also had a reputation for rowdiness and rebellion. They were the anti-Beatles in a lot of ways. Some music critics said that if the Beatles wanted to hold your hand, the Stones wanted to burn your house down. Smith may have sensed the energy—and that rebellion.

As the band started to play, the crush of teenage girls pushed Smith closer and closer to the stage. The surge began to scare Smith, who was afraid she would be trampled to death. The fear became a real possibility as she began to lose her footing. Just as she was about to fall to the floor, she reached out to guitarist Brian Jones, who was sitting at the edge of the stage playing sitar. Smith grabbed hold of Jones's ankle to regain her balance.

She would later comment that the two exchanged glances.

But did something even more significant happen during those few seconds of physical contact between the two artists? Did that simple fleeting connection create a spiritual entanglement between Jones and Smith?

Years later, Smith would experience the soul-to-soul connection with Jones one last, fateful time. In a biography about the singer, Nick Johnstone wrote that Smith had recently been burned after a boiling pot of water was accidentally spilled on her. The pain medication she was taking made her groggy, and she went to sleep. It was a fitful sleep. She awoke after a few hours and began to vomit.

Her sister, who was staying to help her after the accident, rushed to her aid. Smith began to tell her that she'd had a terrible dream about Brian Jones. She said that, in the dream, Jones had died. Smith insisted that the two fly to Paris. When they landed at the airport, a headline of a newspaper immediately caught their attention:

"Brian Jones Mort." Or, in English, "Brian Jones, Dead."

They were too late. The founding member of the Rolling Stones had been found dead in a swimming pool at his mansion. The dream came too late to help their idol, and the sisters were devastated.

For Smith, the prophetic gift turned into a curse. Shortly after her premonition about Jones, Smith began to have dreams about her father. Specifically, she dreamed about her father's heart. The dreams frightened Smith and her sister, who both vowed to return to the States to check on their dad. After Jones's death, the sisters had learned to respect the power of intuition or premonition, or whatever power had helped them reach into the future.

When they got home, they found that their father had suffered a heart attack. Fortunately, he survived and was resting in the hospital. But Smith was once again reminded that there is a fine line between poet and prophet.

SECTION IV

ROCK AND ROLL'S MOST FAMOUS CURSES AND MYSTERIES

People who make it to the top of the rough and callous world of the music industry are often looked on as the blessed, the chosen few. They fought the odds. They played the dives and dead-end bars, honing their sound in front of unruly—or, worse, indifferent—crowds. They beat incompetent and often unscrupulous management, who tried to steal from them and exploit them. They weathered personal tragedies—all in the quest to climb to the top of the charts.

But once they reach those lofty heights, some of rock's most famous artists have found that, far from being blessed by the journey, they're cursed. The curses that haunt our favorite rock stars are numerous and well documented. These curses are typically attached to individuals, but they are also attached to certain musical chords and even poor real estate choices. Even though fans have spent, in some cases, decades hashing and rehashing the details of curses, the causes of these curses are far from settled.

We already discussed Robert Johnson and his deal with the devil. Some would classify Johnson's negotiation with Lucifer as a curse, but it was more like a trade. The devil gave Johnson talent and celebrity in exchange for his soul. The deal was somewhere between a heavenly curse and a diabolical blessing for Johnson. There are rumors that other artists have ventured down that crossroads—or crossed the Devil's Bridge—in the pitch black of night to meet a man with a contract and a pen. His contract has simple terms: you get everything you want, and he gets your soul.

Another curse may have followed one of the biggest supergroups of the 1970s, Led Zeppelin. A series of misfortunes hovered over the band, leading some to speculate that the origin of the curse could be traced back to the magical aspirations of one of its members.

But not all curses come from the magical quests of wannabe rock stars. In this section, we'll look at rock and roll's brightest stars who seem to be cursed for no reason at all. They never made a deal with the devil or conjured up a demon, but the curse seems to follow them like a shadow.

Rock and roll curses often are not punishment for bad behavior, either. In fact, some of rock's most deadly curses revolve around people whom most consider to be among the nicest guys and gals in the entertainment business—like Buddy Holly.

Other rock and roll curses are attached to objects. We'll discover that many friends and family members of Ricky Nelson believe his cursed mansion may have doomed his career and even brought on his untimely, tragic death in a freak airplane accident.

If a mansion can be cursed, how about an apartment? Singer-songwriter Harry Nilsson owned an apartment in London that was the center of two rock star deaths. People say the deaths—and the growing reputation that the apartment was cursed—caused him to sell the place.

Other curses seem to originate from the music itself. In this chapter, we'll hear about a progression of musical notes that is supposedly so diabolical, the Roman Catholic Church banned musicians from using it back in the Middle Ages.

Our first stop on this journey into the cursed realm of rock and roll history starts with probably the most famous tale of bad luck run amok: the curse of Buddy Holly.

CHAPTER 29

THE BUDDY HOLLY CURSE

Thick Glasses and an Even Thicker Mystery

Buddy Holly remains one of the most powerful and positive influences on rock musicians. His talent for crafting simple yet intricately beautiful songs changed the course of rock history and inspired people like John Lennon, Paul McCartney, Mick Jagger, and dozens of others to become singer-songwriters.

Holly was more than a Texan guitar slinger who could belt out a catchy tune; he was a composer and musical arranger who dared to take rock and roll in a new direction. Before Holly, few musicians wrote and performed their own tunes.

Most critics would agree that he was the first rock musician to treat the new musical style as an artform, not as a novelty. Holly used strings and orchestral accompaniments for his songs. He also experimented with multitrack recordings, layering instruments into the musical fabric of his compositions.

To say that Buddy Holly and his band, the Crickets, left an impression on pop culture, generally, and rock music, specifically, is a massive understatement. You can hear his influence in nearly every Beatles song and in band names, like the Hollies. Even the name "the Beatles" is a takeoff on Holly's backup band, "the Crickets." Look at the playlist of any band in the British Invasion and you'll find Holly tunes, like "Rave On," "That'll Be the Day," and "Peggy Sue."

You can even find Holly's influence in modern recording equipment in studios, which has grown up around Holly's idea that rock artists should produce works of art, not just quick hits.

Holly left an impression in other ways, too, and not all good. There are those who suggest that whatever dark cloud followed Buddy Holly's own star-crossed life and career also followed those who were connected to the singer. Shortly after Holly died, the Buddy Holly curse made its initial appearance.

R. Gary Patterson, in his book *Take a Walk on the Dark Side*, lists a few of the victims of Buddy Holly's curse. A rebel guitar player was one of the first.

The Curse Claims Cochran

Eddie Cochran was a fellow rock and roll rebel who became friends with Holly and Ritchie Valens, the young, fast-climbing star who perished in the plane crash during the Winter Dance Party Tour. Cochran was supposed to be on that tour. And that haunted him. Obviously, he was crushed when he heard the news about the crash. Most of his friends told him he should be relieved that he dodged a bullet from the rock and roll curse, but Cochran became deeply afraid that whatever curse had been stalking his friends would come after him. Some of those closest to the guitar player said he obsessed over the deaths, even recording a song, "Three Songs," that paid tribute to his friends, Holly, Valens, and the Big Bopper.

In 1960, Cochran left for a tour of England. It was an open secret that he wanted the tour to be his last. He hoped to wind down his career as a performing artist and concentrate on the much safer occupations of writing songs and producing other artists. Nearing the end of the tour, Cochran, his songwriter girlfriend Sharon Sheeley, and fellow musician Gene Vincent may have fleetingly thought they were home free of the Holly curse as they headed to the airport to catch a flight back to the States.

On the way to the airport, the car they were riding in blew a tire and crashed. Sheeley broke her back and Vincent reinjured his knee. Cochran was thrown from the car and was rushed to the hospital. He died the next day. As Cochran clung to life in the hospital, some unexpected visitors dropped by to pay their respects: Jerry Allison, Sonny Curtis, and Joe B. Mauldin—former members of Holly's backing band, the Crickets—were also in England for a tour.

The list of tragedies connected with the Buddy Holly curse began to pile up after Cochran's crash.

Ronnie Smith was a replacement singer for Buddy Holly as the ill-fated Winter Dance Party Tour continued. Smith was friends with the Crickets and even performed with some of the band members on occasion. His new band included Waylon Jennings, another member of the Holly posse. Soon after the tour with Holly, Smith's life began to unravel in ways that none of his friends or family could have predicted.

It started with substance abuse. He began to use drugs and grew increasingly dependent on them. The abuse became so bad that he was sent to a state mental hospital in Texas, but the treatment and extra help did not help his mental condition. A few months after his admission to the hospital, the severely depressed Smith hanged himself in the hospital.

Although Smith's fans and friends were saddened by the news, they were also confused. How could a musician of such talent and such promise slip to such a low point that he would take his own life?

Some of those—especially fans familiar with the curse—wondered whether Smith wasn't just another victim of the Buddy Holly curse.

Bobby Fuller and the Buddy Holly Curse

Perhaps the most gruesome fate of the Buddy Holly curse awaited Bobby Fuller, frontman for the Holly-influenced Bobby Fuller Four.

Fuller was a Texas native and a huge Buddy Holly fan. His musical gifts and Texas upbringing drew comparisons to Holly. Fuller didn't mind the comparison and, of course, jumped at the chance to work with Norman Petty, Holly's original manager and a man with whom Holly had had a famous falling out.

Despite regional fame, Fuller struggled at getting his band off the ground in Texas. While he enjoyed the solid backing of a hometown crowd, he longed for something bigger. Fuller decided to move the outfit to Hollywood in search of stardom. Fuller's luck really changed when Sonny Curtis, a guitar player for the Crickets, wrote a song for him that would not only be a national hit, but would serve as his signature tune. Fuller's gritty version of "I Fought the Law" swept into the Top Ten. The Buddy Holly influence was unmistakable.

In so many ways, Fuller's career began to mimic Holly's own star-crossed career. Fuller's hit started to bring him a national audience—and an entire globe of fans was waiting. Fuller dropped his backing band and started a solo career—just like Holly. And, just like Holly, a dark cloud appeared on the horizon as soon as Fuller began to skyrocket into superstar status. Fuller recorded his last song, "Love's Made a Fool of You." The song was written by Buddy Holly.

The song would prove prophetic.

Accounts vary, but most of the stories about that fateful night agree that at 1:00 a.m. on July 18, 1966, Fuller answered a phone call. The call seemed urgent, according to his mother, who shared the Hollywood apartment with the singer. Fuller left the apartment in a hurry—and never came back.

The next day, Fuller was supposed to meet his guitar player, who had recently been drafted into the military. The guitarist planned to sell his car to Fuller. When word of the no-show began to filter through the band mates and friends who hung out in Fuller's circle, the apprehension grew.

It wasn't exactly like Fuller to miss a meeting. On the other hand, most of the group knew that Fuller's fascination with LSD and psychedelics had pulled him closer and closer into the seamier side of Los Angeles's nightlife, an odd mix of philosophers, artists, druggies, and prostitutes. There were even hints that Fuller was hanging out with members of organized crime.

While the band members agonized over Fuller's disappearance, his mother organized a search. Later in the afternoon, Fuller's Oldsmobile was spotted. In fact, the car had mysteriously reappeared—parked in front of the apartment.

The mystery was just starting. Fuller's gasoline-soaked body was found in the car. Some witnesses said that Fuller's body had bruises and showed other signs of struggle, or violence. One witness said the singer's fingers were broken. Despite this, the Los Angeles police quickly ruled the death a suicide. To many of Fuller's friends and family, that made no sense. Fuller was not unhappy and was coming into his own musically. In fact, he appeared to be going in a new musical direction. The gasoline? Who tries to commit suicide by drinking gasoline? Most of the people close to Fuller vehemently rejected the police's verdict on the death. They smelled a coverup.

Rumors continued to swirl about the untimely death, and other competing, more lurid theories started to circulate. The bruises? The gasoline? The connections to the nightclub scene? Many familiar with the case said it had all the signs of a mob hit. Maybe the mobsters had soaked Fuller in gasoline because they were planning on torching the car and Fuller's body. The signs of a struggle—bruises and broken bones—may indicate that Fuller put up a fight. The conspiracy theorists offered more evidence. The mob was active in the Los Angeles music scene. Many clubs that Fuller played at and frequented were connected to the mob.

There was another theory that Fuller wasn't killed because of drugs or money, he was killed because love really made a fool out of him. According to this variation of the story, Fuller was involved in a romantic tryst with a mobster's girlfriend, or at least the girlfriend of someone—perhaps a club owner—connected with the mob. Fuller was whacked to end the relationship.

The behavior of Fuller's circle of musicians and friends appears to support the notion that nefarious elements were at work in Fuller's death, or murder—and they weren't done just yet. Several band mates fled the L.A. music scene and went to Texas. They were packing pistols, too. There were other rumors that armed men showed up at Fuller's apartment after his death, an obvious message to any potential witness who might have been thinking of squealing to the cops.

Even if a witness did go to the police, there's no telling whose side the cops would have been on. Many questioned the police investigation. Why were they so quick to label it a suicide? Were they paid off by the mob?

Maybe Fuller fought the law and the mob—and the mob won.

A mob hit wasn't the only conjecture about Fuller's death. Another theory is that he went to a party that night and took too many drugs. The other partygoers panicked when Fuller died and tried to cover up the mishap. If that's true, they failed miserably.

The last theory about Fuller's death was simple: he succumbed to the Buddy Holly curse.

A Runaway Curse

Del Shannon was a singer-songwriter whose career was molded by Holly. Just listen to his hit "Little Runaway" and you'll hear all of the elements—driving rhythm, infectious melody, and lush harmonies—that define a Holly song.

Shannon never shied away from the comparisons to Holly and never tried to hide his admiration for the Lubbock sensation. On February 3, 1990, Shannon even appeared at an anniversary concert for Buddy Holly. He was backed by none other than the original Crickets band.

Just five days later, Shannon killed himself, yet another victim of the Holly curse.

The Norman Petty Curse?

For the truly conspiracy-minded, the strange deaths and misfortunes of Buddy Holly, Eddie Cochran, the Big Bopper, Ritchie Valens, Bobby Fuller, and others aren't the result of the Buddy Holly curse, but the Norman Petty curse.

Petty was a record producer and manager in Texas when he met Buddy Holly. He took on the young singer as his producer and manager. It wasn't a happy relationship. Holly claimed that Petty cheated him out of thousands of dollars. Critics claimed that Petty added his name as a co-writer to hits that Holly had written all by himself. Threats of lawsuits and countersuits flew when Perry, Holly, and Holly's wife met for the last time just before Holly's tour.

Whether this bad blood caused a curse to develop between the two men isn't clear. What is clear, however, is that Holly had to go on the ill-fated winter tour in large part to make up for the money he lost to Petty.

Fuller and Petty, too, had their share of run-ins. Petty was not happy to lose Fuller when he left for California. He considered Fuller his next Buddy Holly. In many ways, he was. Fuller met just as violent an end—and just as tragic—as Holly. He was about a year older than Holly when he was doomed to die. Or, should I say, he was about a year older than Holly when he was cursed to die.

So was it the Holly curse or the Petty curse? That debate, unlike the music that died on February 3, 1959, will not die.

CHAPTER 30

RICKY NELSON:

Did a Former Teen Idol Fall Victim to the Curse of a Haunted House?

Before the 1980s, if you were going to lay money down on which celebrity would end up cursed, you wouldn't have put a dime on Ricky Nelson. That guy had it all.

He was born into a family of celebrities. His father, Ozzie, was a well-known, well-liked, and well-respected musician and actor who helped pioneer the fledgling television entertainment industry. Before he was even in his teens, Ricky was a celebrity, starring with his father, mother, and brother in the early television smash hit *The Adventures of Ozzie and Harriet*. The program defined what a sitcom was and lasted almost fourteen years. At age thirteen, Ricky was making $100,000 a year.

During the height of his fame as a teen actor, Ricky turned to rock music—which, like his own career, was coming into its own. With Ricky's natural talent, backed by the exposure of the sitcom, he became an instant rock star. Following on the heels of his hero, Elvis Presley, he belted out a string of hits, like "Poor Little Fool" and "Be-Bop Baby."

Like I said, the kid had it all.

Just two decades later, though, before he died in a mysterious fire on a plane he had chartered for a tour, Ricky's life was a tangled mess of debt, divorce, and drugs.

So what happened?

Some friends and family members say they know exactly what happened—a haunted house happened. And the spirit in that house cursed him. According to those closest to the singer, a dark cloud began to blot out the light of this once luminous star when Ricky and his family moved into the estate formerly owned by Errol Flynn, equally well known for being an actor and a Hollywood badass. What the family may not have known is that the mansion had a reputation for being even more badass than Flynn.

There are lots of Hollywood mansions that host spirits, but the ghosts who haunt them are usually friendly, or at least not homicidal. That wasn't the case with Flynn's mansion on Mulholland Farm. People who stayed in the place said that they would see glasses fly off of tables and shatter on the floor. Chairs would sail across the room like they were made of matchsticks. No one was even close to the objects to create this type of havoc.

Most paranormal researchers would suggest that these types of activities are classic signs that a poltergeist is operating in the home. But they add that poltergeists are usually attached to a human being, whom they refer to as the "agent." The human—unwittingly, in most cases—is using telekinetic powers to shatter glass and toss chairs around. Poltergeists essentially haunt humans, not houses. If the human agent leaves a place, typically the phenomena disappear with him or her. If that's so, then who was the agent in Flynn's home? Flynn was long dead, but the spooky phenomena kept happening.

A better guess, paranormal experts would say, is that an evil entity was haunting the mansion. In fact, most believe that the mansion's evil entity had a name. It was Errol Flynn.

Ricky didn't seem to care.

And to be honest, despite his clean-cut looks and big, fancy house, Ricky had a bit of a badass reputation himself. He joined a greasers gang in high school. He was booed off a Madison Square Garden stage during a rock and roll review show when he refused to play his old hits, instead sticking to his new material. Ricky wasn't the type of guy who was going to be scared by a ghost of some old-timey actor.

Ricky's son Gunnar and his daughter, Tracy, said in several interviews that the house had a malevolent vibe, something that they had sensed immediately. After living in the mansion for a few months, the family could see changes in Ricky's demeanor. Gunnar said that the home's dark energy seemed to consume his father. Tracy agreed with that, adding that the move into the home appeared to match a slide in her father's personal and professional fortunes.

It wasn't just a feeling. The paranormal activity began to ramp up, too. Most of the family reported experiencing strange phenomena. The shower door would open and close. Window shades would spring up even though there was no one near the window. Often, before a manifestation, Tracy recalled smelling cheap perfume. At times, especially when she was alone, Tracy also detected a sinister, cynical presence.

The mansion was like a reverse fun house. Its hidden rooms and passageways were legendary. The mansion was also outfitted with peepholes and two-way mirrors, perfect for spying on the sexual hijinks that routinely occurred during parties. According to biographers, Flynn or one of his associates would lure an unsuspecting starlet into a bedroom while others in rooms behind the two-way mirrors or peepholes watched.

One day, Gunnar was going about his daily routine when he thought he saw a fleeting image in the mirror. It made Ricky's son do a double take. When he looked back, a man's face was staring right back at him. Then it was gone. A little historical investigation revealed that the mirror where Gunnar had seen the face was located near one of the infamous peepholes.

The family seemed powerless to stop Ricky's descent into darkness. If Ricky ever experienced the entity, or ever witnessed any of the paranormal activity, he never spoke about it. According to family members, the fact that Ricky never admitted the home was haunted may not be so unbelievable, because even though he seemed to be the focus of the haunting, the paranormal force that gripped the mansion was affecting him in other, more subtle yet equally devastating ways.

On December 31, 1985, the DC-3 that carried Ricky and his band on their short tour of the southern United States crash-landed. Witnesses said a fire quickly spread through the plane. Some even speculated that the plane was on fire before it took off.

But before we cast blame for Ricky's death on the mansion or Errol Flynn, we should mention another rumor: the crash was the result of another rock and roll curse. Ricky performed one last song during an encore before jumping on his chartered plane, according to several sources. That song? "Rave On," a Buddy Holly classic.

CHAPTER 31

THE BEASTLY CURSE:

A Rock Supergroup's Trouble with the Super Evil

Jimmy Page was a wizard on the guitar.

Even before he became the lead guitar player for Led Zeppelin, he was a musical prodigy who showed off his skiffle guitar playing on television when he was just a kid. Then he attained near legendary status as a highly sought-after session player—a musician whom solo acts and bands hire for recording sessions. Page played guitar on albums for bands who were already known for their guitar players, bands like the Who and the Kinks. But they paid to have Page play on their albums because he added something to a song—something intangible, something magical.

Despite the good pay as a session player and, later, his fame as the lead guitarist for one of the most successful rock groups of the 1970s, Page wanted more. He admitted he wasn't content with being a guitar wizard; he wanted to become an actual wizard.

Led Zeppelin's guitar-playing sorcerer was a fan of occult wizard Aleister Crowley, who practically terrorized England in the late nineteenth and early twentieth centuries. Crowley was better known by his nicknames (which he relished) "666" or "the Beast." He was much more fond of the moniker "the wickedest man in the world," a nickname he strove to live up to every day. Page studied Crowley's lengthy and obscure books. As we discussed in an earlier chapter, he even bought the mansion once owned—and reportedly haunted—by Crowley.

Some of the band's fans—and even some rock historians—would not refer to Page's fascination with the occult as a spiritual connection, though. They'd call it a curse.

For Zep fans, the curse is well known and ignites fiery debates about the band. Some fans say the Led Zep curse was responsible for several misfortunes and deaths that seemed to stalk the band as it rose to superstardom during the late 1970s. Other fans say all of the misfortunes and tragedies are nothing more than coincidence.

For those in the "Zep is cursed" camp, the effects of the curse started to show after the band formed in late 1968. In 1975, for instance, lead singer Robert Plant took members of his family along with Scarlet Page, Jimmy Page's daughter, for a ride on the island of Rhodes, a Greek island that was—and still is—a popular tourist destination. The scenic auto ride turned tragic. Plant's wife, who was driving the rental car, lost control and wrecked the vehicle. The only member of the group who wasn't injured was Page's daughter.

More tragedies, which seemed aimed at Led Zeppelin members, followed.

While the band was touring America in 1977, Robert Plant's son died from what doctors termed an extremely rare respiratory condition. More misfortunes followed. John Bonham was in a car wreck and broke several ribs. A year later, Keith Moon, the Who's iconoclastic drummer and the person who supposedly gave Led Zeppelin their name, overdosed and died.

Then, on September 25, 1980, just as the troubled waters seemed to calm for the band, Bonham died after a raucous night of drinking, a night that ironically was meant to celebrate the rebirth of Led Zep. Bonham died in Page's home.

These were just the biggies—the list of other deaths and suicides of Led Zep friends, managers, and associates is long. Some victims aren't even directly connected to the band; they just happened to unwittingly tempt the curse's retributive powers.

In the late 1970s, Eddie and the Hot Rods was an up-and-coming English rock band, who may have run afoul of the Led Zep curse. Just like Led Zeppelin, Eddie and the Hot Rods was influenced by Crowley and his occult writings. The band decided to record a song based on Crowley's most famous precept, "Do what thou wilt shall be the whole of the law." Their catchy little ditty was "Do Anything You Wanna Do."

The tune hit the Top Ten. So far, so good. But then, according to some occult rock historians, Eddie and the Hot Rods got a little cocky. On a whim, for the artwork on the song's cover sleeve, they had a picture of Crowley wearing Mickey Mouse ears. This was no way to pay homage to the Beast. Rumor has it that this disrespectful cover reached Page himself, who was none too happy.

For Eddie and the Hot Rods, the fame and fortune that appeared so tantalizingly close vanished in an instant. Their manager became hooked on heroin. Their label dropped them. They never even got close to the top of the charts again.

Blogger Peter Watts said that Paul Gray, bassist for the band, believes there was a connection between the bad breaks and the poor choice in cover. He told Watts, in no uncertain terms, that "weird shit happened after that. A lot of people said we shouldn't have fucked about with Crowley."

Not all are convinced about the curse. There are those who say that the list of misfortunes that haunted Led Zeppelin wasn't the result of any type of heavy-metal mumbo jumbo. Cooking up a rock and roll curse story is a two-ingredient recipe that's easy and simple to follow: one part coincidence and one part hard-living, super-risky rock and roll lifestyle. After all, the real evil spirits that caused Bonham's death were the reported forty shots of vodka he consumed that night.

There's nothing strange about probability, the skeptics say. If you increase your risky behavior, you increase the chances that bad things will happen. The Led Zeppelin curse is nothing more than a study of risk management gone awry.

But believers in the Led Zep curse call attention to one strange fact: Page was never touched by the tragedy.

They wonder if Page wasn't somehow protected from the curse, or maybe he actually was the source.

CHAPTER 32

THE DEVIL'S INTERVAL: Rock's Cursed Chord

It didn't take long for the sinuous rhythms of rock and roll to create a group of religious and cultural critics who immediately questioned the merits of the new musical form. It didn't take these critics long to start questioning the musical origins of rock, either. Where did this music come from? Better question: Who started it?

Religious critics had an immediate answer: rock music came from hell. It was quickly labeled the devil's music by preachers and pastors who implored the young faithful from their flocks to stay away from this new music sensation that was sweeping the country.

It wasn't the first time that music was labeled demonic, or satanic. But some of rock's religious foes said that they could prove that rock and roll had diabolical roots and that musicians knowingly manipulated the chords of their songs to accomplish the grandest of devilish deeds: to summon the devil himself. The notes are dubbed the devil's interval, or the devil's chord.

To find the devil's interval, you just slightly twist the major scale, the scale that most non-devil-worshipping Western songwriters and composers use to construct their melodies and harmonies. It's easiest to use the C-major scale to understand the interval. C major uses all the white keys on a piano to play the notes: C, D, E, F, G, A, B, and back to C. Each white key represents a step.

The black keys on the piano represent half steps. The first thing you notice is that there are black keys missing between the E and F notes and between the B and C notes. That is because the major scale is not symmetrical. There are half steps between E and F, and B and C, whereas there are whole steps between the other notes in the scale, like between F and G, and G and A.

But what happens if you play only whole steps in the C-major scale? In other words, what happens if you play C, D, E, and F sharp (G flat), G sharp (A flat), A sharp (B flat), and then back to C? Instead of a seven-note scale, this is a symmetrical six-note scale. And it sounds a little creepy.

Then listen to two notes of the scale—C and F sharp (G flat)—played together. Most people say the sound gives them an unsettling feeling. If you play the notes one at a time, you might be reminded of the famous guitar intro for Jimi Hendrix's psychedelic hit "Purple Haze." That intro was so gripping that most rock fans can tell you exactly where they were when they first heard that biting guitar chip away at the devil's interval on the radio, stereo, or MP3 player. The question is, what—or who—was doing the gripping?

The devil's chord also uses three whole tones with an augmented fourth.

In fact, the secret of the devil's chord and devil's interval is much older—and much more diabolical—than this modern manifestation of the opening notes of "Purple Haze." In the 1700s, Giuseppe Tartini, a violinist and composer, said Satan himself helped him create his "Devil's Trill Sonata" using the devil's interval. Most violinists will tell you that the piece is particularly complex and difficult to learn.

"Danse Macabre," which is Camille Saint-Saens's sinister-sounding salute to the dead coming alive on Halloween, makes generous use of the diminished fifth, in which the fifth note of a scale is lowered by a half step. Richard Wagner, Germany's famous composer, used the devil's interval, too.

Franz Liszt, the Hungarian composer and piano virtuoso, used this six-note scale, called the tritone scale, in his compositions. The imagery that went with several of his compositions, like the Mephisto Waltzes, was filled with scenes of the devil playing the violin and dancing.

The rumor is that some of Liszt's pieces were inspired by master violinist Niccolo Paganini. Paganini might have been the original contract signer at the crossroads. The Italian came from a poor family, and not an especially musical one. But almost overnight, the young man could play the violin like no one else.

When people watched Paganini play violin, they were amazed by the music that he conjured from the instrument. But it wasn't just the music. For the shocked audiences that flocked to his performances, the violinist played like he was mad, or, as the more religious would describe, like he was possessed. He writhed. He swayed. He stomped and dipped.

Rumors spread that Paganini was possessed—and not by a love of music. In the minds of nineteenth-century Europeans, there was only one way to explain Paganini's talent: he was possessed by the devil. In each city that Paganini played, stories were whispered that he had acquired such talent by selling his soul to the devil.

Some occult theorists speculate that would-be violinists and rock stars don't have to travel to crossroads at some ungodly hour to wait for the devil; they can summon the devil with a few notes of their violin or guitar. Musicians, rumor has it, just strike those simple notes of the tritone scale in a certain way to summon the devil. That's when the deals for fame and fortune are struck.

The devil's interval was so diabolically powerful that the Roman Catholic Church allegedly banned its use in the Middle Ages. Church authorities backed up the ban under threat of torture, according to some musicologists.

When rock and roll got hold of the devil's interval, churches began to revive their claims that the bands were trying to raise hell—literally. Black Sabbath guitarist Tony Iommi masterfully used the devil's interval in the band's devilish debut album. But Iommi swears his innocence in using the music to summon the devil.

Iommi told the British newspaper *The Guardian*, "I didn't think I was going to make devil music. It was just something that sounded right." Despite his protests of innocence in attempting to summon the devil through his own brand of rock music, it's important to note that Iommi did call both his band and the band's debut album "Black Sabbath."

And, obviously, a guy who names his band after a satanic rite would have no interest in summoning the devil with a guitar riff, right?

CHAPTER 33

ON TOUR, PERMANENTLY:

Did Aliens Abduct a Future Rock Star?

In 1975, search parties began to scour the desert around the outskirts of Santa Rosa, New Mexico, a town situated on rock and roll's historic Route 66 and about two hours north of the supposed UFO crash site in Roswell, New Mexico.

The team was searching for Jim Sullivan, a budding rock star, who disappeared without a trace. They found his car and his guitar, but they never found Sullivan, which makes some rock and roll folklorists speculate that nobody found a body because someone—from beyond—found him first.

Sullivan was a musician and actor who was one break away from stardom. He had a cameo in the counterculture flick *Easy Rider*, starring Peter Fonda, Dennis Hopper, and Jack Nicholson. Sullivan's 1969 album, *U.F.O.*, received some critical acclaim, and also revealed the singer-songwriter's interest in alien intelligences.

The title cut of the album clearly touched on what was becoming a cultural phenomenon in the United States—and almost an obsession in the rock and roll community: unidentified flying objects, or UFOs. By the time Sullivan was penning tunes about flying spacecraft, Jimi Hendrix and members of the Byrds had gone on record as UFO nuts (not UFO-nauts; there's a difference). Sullivan's album lyrics seem to talk about a man who leaves his family and is abducted by aliens in the desert. These may not be just song lyrics, though; they may be a prophecy.

Despite the bit parts in movies and the acclaim that was building for his music, fame proved elusive for Sullivan, who became convinced his ticket to stardom would require a stop to Nashville, home of some of the best musicians of that time. He planned to drive across the country and meet up with some of these pickers who would help him reestablish his career. Leaving his wife and family behind, Sullivan jumped in his car and began his cross-country trek to Music City.

While it's impossible to know this for certain, it may have occurred to Sullivan, a UFO believer, that his route would take him directly through the hottest UFO spots in the country. The American Southwest, with its sparse population, clear skies, and wide-open vistas, make it one of the best places in the United States to chase UFOs.

Although mainstream focus on UFOs was still a few years away, the 1947 Roswell incident was drawing more attention from UFO buffs at the time of Sullivan's trip. In fact, Sullivan may have read about or studied the reported crash landing of a spacecraft on a ranch in the New Mexico desert.

Maybe that's why they found Sullivan's car pulled over in the desert. He may have been watching for alien craft. But certain members of the UFO community had another idea: Sullivan may have been watching for aliens. But what if the aliens were watching him? Some believe that there was no trace of Sullivan's disappearance because he was abducted. As proof, they mention that Sullivan's property in the car was not disturbed, and there was no sign of a struggle.

The biggest piece of evidence had six strings. When the searchers discovered Sullivan's car, they noticed that the guitar was still inside. If Sullivan decided he was going to vanish and start a new life somewhere else, wouldn't he want to take his guitar? It was probably his meal ticket.

As record label owner Matt Sullivan told National Public Radio in a recent interview: "One thing that one of Jim's friends pointed out was that the guitar was left in the car. If Jim was going to disappear, that would have been the one thing that he would have taken, because wherever he was in the world, he could always stand on a street corner and make a few bucks playing his guitar."

Besides the guitar and the lack of a crime scene, people wondered why Sullivan would want to leave his friends, family, and career behind, especially when he was making the trip to Nashville to secure his fame. People who are hoping to be famous don't decide the next day to disappear.

Only a few facts are known about the disappearance. Early in the day, a police officer did notice Sullivan's vehicle swerving on the road. The cop pulled the musician over. Sullivan explained that he had been driving for several hours straight and was falling asleep. The officer gave Sullivan a warning and directed him to a nearby motel, where he could catch up on his sleep.

Not all the theories are based on alien abductions. The mob was fairly active in the region. He may have gotten in an argument with a mobster and ended up paying the ultimate price. The desert isn't just a great place to land a UFO, it's also a great place to bury a body.

But for many conspiracy-minded folks, that prophetic song is too uncannily descriptive of the actual incident. They say if you want the key to Sullivan's disappearance, just listen to that song and look at those lyrics. And then look up at the stars.

CHAPTER 34

MUSICLAND STUDIOS:
Bad Breezes and Evil Vibrations

In previous chapters, we talked about studios that were haunted. But can studios be cursed, too? Some rock stars will tell you that one studio in Germany is definitely cursed.

Based on the long list of rock and disco stars who strutted into Musicland Studios in Munich and turned their tunes into gold and platinum during the 1970s and 1980s, you would never guess that the building harbored a dark, sinister secret. The artists all seemed lucky enough. The Rolling Stones, Led Zeppelin, Donna Summer, and Elton John, to name a few, recorded monster hits at the facility.

But some of these artists, who had their coffers filled with the money made in Musicland Studios, also whispered that the place was cursed. In fact, some said it was an ancient curse.

Brian May, guitar player for Queen, was one of the artists who recorded in the studio. He sensed something diabolical about Musicland, which was built in the basement of a high-rise building. In an interview, he said that when Queen recorded a few songs and a video at Musicland, he never felt comfortable. Maybe it was the isolation. There were no windows, no natural lighting. The studio was depressing and felt like a bunker, at least to the guitarist.

He also heard rumors that the building had attracted more than its share of suicide victims. Several people had jumped off the top of the building, according to the stories that filtered through the band during the recording sessions.

It might also not just be a coincidence that Jimmy Page—who was often accompanied by darker spirits and whispered suggestions of malevolent curses—spent some time at Musicland. Was he the source of the curse? The Led Zep curse did seem to spin into overtime right after the band laid down tracks at Musicland.

May never blamed Page, but he and others suggested another form of curse might be responsible for the negative energy he picked up at the studio. In Germany, he said, there's a strange wind called "the föhn." Föhn winds, common in certain areas of Europe, are breezes that blow down the slopes of mountains. The warm breezes are known for their ability to melt snow rapidly. It's a common meteorological phenomenon in the area, but when people watch the breezes melt away snow piles almost instantly, it may appear that an evil spirit is exhaling its hot breath over the land.

That may be one reason that föhn winds have gotten such an evil reputation, and, since Musicland was built where the bizarre breezes are prevalent, it's natural to assume that the rumor would get wrapped up in the notion that the studio is cursed.

But there may actually be some proof that a curse is at work. Some research suggests that föhn breezes increase the likelihood of migraines and even psychosis. Perhaps this is the reason why people have decided to leap off the building that Musicland used to call home.

The studio, by the way, is no longer there. But it wasn't a curse that led to its demise. It was bad vibrations of another sort that forced Musicland Studios to relocate. A new subway system, built near the studio, hurt the recording quality.

CHAPTER 35

FLAT CURSED:

Harry Nilsson's Bad Real Estate Mojo

For a guy with a reputation for negative mojo, Harry Nilsson had a somewhat charmed career.

The singer-songwriter, who was born to Swedish circus performers, never toured and never even played a major concert. Nilsson didn't need throngs of fans to be a rock star. He had a following from some of the most impressive names in the music business, including Phil Spector and the Beatles.

Despite any push of his own to create a career or capitalize on this fame, Nilsson won a cult following, critical acclaim, numerous industry awards—and whispered rumors that misfortune followed the publicity-shy Nilsson the way some groupies traipsed after other adoration-seeking rock stars.

The epicenter of the Nilsson curse is the flat that he once owned in London. It was not the scene of just one rock star death, but two. Nilsson bought the flat on Curzon Street on the outskirts of the Mayfair district in London because of its close proximity to Apple Studio, the studio made famous by the Beatles. Oh, who am I kidding? He bought the flat because it was also walking distance from discos and, especially, the Playboy Club. Nilsson was a walking and, more often than not, staggering contradiction: he shied away from performing publicly but was also an attention-seeking party animal when he hit the town.

Nilsson's flat became a hangout for a few of his friends and a staging ground for their nightly activities. When friends came to London, they often crashed at Nilsson's flat for extended periods of time. In 1974, Cass Elliot, who was once a member of the Mamas and the Papas, asked the songwriter if she could stay at Nilsson's pad while she performed shows as a solo act at the London Palladium. A ticket to one of Elliot's shows was *the* ticket to have during the summer concert season. She was wowing the crowds.

On July 29, Elliot was in rare form, belting out one classic after another. The audience loved it. She roared through the performance and then through several encores. At the end of the show, Elliot said she was exhausted and hurried back to the flat to rest up. It appeared like a routine night for the singer, but later, Elliot was found dead in the bedroom. The coroner said she died of heart failure. She was only thirty-two.

A few years later, Nilsson lent a room to yet another friend and drinking partner. This time he handed over the apartment keys to mercurial rocker Keith Moon, drummer and chief nut for the Who. Moon and his girlfriend, Annette Walter-Lax, were staying in Nilsson's flat in September of 1978. His girlfriend said he woke up and asked her to cook a steak for him.

She complained, and Moon said what were to be his last words: "If you don't like it, you can fuck off."

Moon took too many clomethiazole pills—a medicine prescribed to help him quit drinking—and never woke up, police said. Only Keith Moon would overdose on a pill aimed to curb his overindulgence. It was typical Moon. There were other reports that Moon died in the exact same bed in which Elliot had passed away just a few years earlier.

I bet I know what you're thinking: if Elliot and Moon died in the same place, were there any ghost stories? The answer is: none that I could find. There are no tales of ghosts roaming the rooms of the famous London flat, or chasing after Nilsson, looking for revenge. There's no sign that Moon's or Cass's spirits are hanging around, at least not in this apartment. The paranormal trail goes cold after Moon's death. It is true that Nilsson, after a second friend died in the flat, was distraught. He may also have been trying to tamp down rumors that he was some sort of jinx—an innuendo that was rapidly spreading though his inner circle of friends and fans. He sold the flat to Pete Townshend, Moon's band mate in the Who. Obviously Pete didn't worry about ghosts.

The Nilsson curse—at least the curse of his flat—seems to end when Townshend bought it. No reports have surfaced of additional tragedies at the once-popular hangout for swinging Londoners.

If you're starting to notice a theme among the rock and roll curses, you're not alone. Many people theorize that this isn't a Nilsson curse at all. A closer look at Moon's death, for instance, indicates that Nilsson may be innocent. It's possible that Moon was yet another victim of another one of rock and roll's famous curses that we've already discussed.

The night before Moon died, he and Walter-Lax went to a movie premiere with Paul and Linda McCartney. The name of the movie? *The Buddy Holly Story.*

CHAPTER 36

CROSSROADS CURSE:
Just Sign on the Demonic Line

In an earlier chapter on bluesman Robert Johnson's ghost, we talked about the legend of the crossroads.

There are several variations on this folkloric theme, but the most common version of the legend states that if a guitarist—or any musician, really—visits the spot where two roads cross at midnight, he—or she (the devil is not sexist)—will meet a man dressed in black.

And we're not talking about Johnny Cash. We're talking about the devil.

The first thing the devil does is take the musician's instrument and tune it up. Then he runs through a few songs. When the devil hands back the instrument, the musician is suddenly and inexplicably able to play any type of blues song, run through the most complex chord changes, and wail through the most intricate solos. But the devil isn't quite done.

He doesn't give fame and fortune away for free. This is a bargain, after all. And, just like the crossroads where the deal gets done, this offer is a two-way deal. Satan gives a little; the musician gives a lot. The devil then proffers a contract. The terms of that contract are simple. The person become an incredibly talented musician, and—after a certain amount of time—the devil comes to repossess his or her soul.

But it wasn't just Johnson who claimed to have made a deal at the crossroads. Lots of musicians have whispered behind the backs of colleagues whose talents blossomed overnight, without any visible effort or extensive period of practice. Other musicians just come out and say they did the deal. In Martin Scorsese's biopic about Bob Dylan, *No Direction Home*, the enigmatic singer-songwriter made reference to his own trip to the crossroads.

According to his friends and fellow musicians whom Scorsese interviewed for the documentary, Dylan was considered just an average folk singer and guitar player when he lived in Minnesota. Nothing special about him. Then one day, Dylan—and the modicum of talent he had—was gone. He vanished from the scene, just like a certain Mississippi bluesman we know. The explanation was that he traveled to New York City, and, you can bet, there are more than a few crossroads between Minnesota and New York.

A few months later, Dylan reappeared on the music scene of his home state, but now he wasn't just another struggling guitar picker. He had mastered dozens of intricate musical styles. His songwriting had matured, too. Somehow, Dylan was writing songs with power and authenticity far beyond his years and experience. Civil rights advocates wondered how a middle-class, white, Jewish kid from Hibbing, Minnesota, could sum up the struggle for equal rights in an eloquently simple song like "Blowing in the Wind."

No one could understand this transformation.

Dylan has an easy explanation: he—like dozens of other famous musicians—said he went to the crossroads. He even admitted later in interviews that this was the reason for his transformation. Whatever deal Dylan signed, he got good terms from the devil. Dylan has had one of the longest careers of anyone who's made that crossroads deal.

The Magical Origins of the Crossroads

For Johnson, the crossroads legend has a geographic center—most say it's at the junction of Highways 61 and 49, near Clarksdale, Mississippi. The legend has a mythic center, too.

Crossroads are considered sacred in many magical traditions. They are places of intense power—and danger. The spot where two roads meet is geographically a place "between two lands." Symbolically, the crossroads is a netherworld between heaven and hell, a place of lost souls.

To trace this idea that crossroads are places of power, we have to venture into ancient mythology. One of the first references is in Greek myth. Hecate, a Greek goddess, ruled the crossroads. In the Voodoo tradition—a mixture of African and Catholic spirituality—many spells and magical incantations must be performed at a crossroads to be effective. Writings from the Middle Ages reveal that people believed that witch groups, or covens, met at crossroads. Crossroads were once considered proper burial spots for dead criminals and suicide victims because the intersecting roads created a crude cross that offered protection from these potentially restless spirits.

It only makes sense that Johnson would make his deal with the devil at the crossroads.

Another Crossroads Curse

The legend that a deal negotiated with the devil at a crossroads quickly turns fame into misfortune is a well-discussed story for blues fans and folklorists, but there's another mystery of the crossroads. Many believe that Johnson's song "Cross Road Blues" is itself cursed.

According to the legend, deal or no crossroads deal, musicians who record the song tend to suffer misfortunes. Johnson, obviously, was the first victim. He died a horrible death; the bluesman—who many say was poisoned by a jealous lover—became ill one night after a visit to a juke joint. He shook violently and vomited throughout the night. The sickness was long and painful, lasting three days, until Johnson finally and mercifully died.

The Allman Brothers were proud to carry on the Southern blues lineage, a path blazed by Johnson, although the band did it with their own Southern-fried rock twist. Reports are that the band loved Johnson's work and performed "Cross Road Blues" many times in concert. Coincidentally—or not—the band endured a string of misfortunes that many blame on the Cross Road Blues curse. Duane Allman died from injuries he sustained in a motorcycle wreck just a few days shy of Halloween in 1971. Duane had been riding his bike in Macon, Georgia, when he swerved to avoid a truck at a crossroads. Almost a year later, Allman Brothers band member Berry

Oakley was riding his motorcycle not too far from the site where Duane crashed when he crashed. Oakley died as well. The connections between the two deaths test the bounds of coincidence.

Musicologists say that Duane's brother, Greg Allman, noted the odd connection between his brother's death and the crossroads in the song "Melissa," writing, "Crossroads, will you ever let him go? Or will you hide the dead man's ghost?"

Eric Clapton, who performed one of the most electric versions of "Cross Road Blues" when he was in the supergroup Cream, reportedly fell under the curse. Just as the band's rendition of the song became popular, Clapton descended into a heroin addiction that almost killed him and sidelined his career for years. In 1991, Clapton's four-year-old son was killed when he fell out of a bedroom window in a Manhattan apartment building.

Was the curse of "Cross Road Blues" behind these tragedies?

There are those who ask the same question about the misfortunes that dogged Lynyrd Skynyrd, one of the most popular Southern rock bands.

The members of Skynyrd enjoyed their own rowdy rock renditions of Robert Johnson songs, including "Cross Road Blues." Like a few other bands that performed the song, Skynyrd's career was marred by a number of misfortunes that fit with the Cross Road Blues curse. In the mid-1970s, the band became one of the most popular rock acts, translating authentic-sounding Southern rock and energetic live performances into multiplatinum albums and sold-out arena concerts. In 1977, at the crest of their fame, the plane that the band had chartered ran out of fuel as it flew to Louisiana. The pilots attempted an emergency landing at a small airport but were unsuccessful.

The plane crashed into a forest near Gillsburg, Mississippi. The pilots, assistant road manager Dean Kilpatrick, and three band members—Ronnie Van Zant, Steve Gaines, and Cassie Gaines—died in the crash.

We talked about the Led Zep curse, but could those series of misfortunes also be related to the Robert Johnson–linked crossroads curse? Singer Robert Plant idolized the late blues singer. He generously lifted Johnson's lyrics for his own songs. The band loved to play "Cross Road Blues," too, as a salute to their fellow crossroads traveler. Misfortunes—deaths, addictions, accidents, and illnesses—soon followed the band.

Some believers in the crossroads curse say that the victims continue to pile up. The latest was Kurt Cobain, the leader of the grunge music movement in the early 1990s. Cobain had played "Cross Road Blues" for his own entertainment for years, those familiar with the case say. He liked to play the tune acoustically. That's the authentic way to play a Johnson song.

The song could have made it onto the Nirvana playlist or even an album. Cobain was reworking the song.

But it wasn't meant to be.

If there is a crossroads curse and Cobain fell under it, it claimed him before he had a chance to popularize Johnson's classic song. He killed himself with a shotgun.

Dylan, who did a version of "Cross Road Blues" called "Down the Highway" on his second album, seems to have dodged the crossroads curse, though it may be because he didn't perform the original version.

The Devil's Bridge

The devil doesn't just hang out at crossroads—that seems to be an American thing. In Europe, you'll likely find the devil making deals on a bridge.

There are dozens of sites called "the Devil's Bridge" in Europe, and, just like the American crossroads counterpart, legends claim that the bridges are meeting places for people who want to trade a favor—like fame and fortune—for their souls. The devil is happy to oblige.

In many of these stories, the bridge itself is a result of a bargain with dark forces. The devil appears to villagers one day and promises to build a bridge for them. Remember, at the time, bridges were enormous engineering projects that required lots of time, talent, and treasure. Bridges have big benefits, too. A bridge can be a big economic boost for villagers, allowing them to easily move goods and crops to other markets. In return for this construction project, the devil asks for the first soul that crosses the bridge.

That's a great story, but what does it have to do with rock and roll?

A lot of those Devil's Bridges are located in England, including one rumored to be in Liverpool, hometown of the world-famous Beatles. There are some rock and roll folklorists who believe that this is no coincidence: the Beatles—or, specifically, John Lennon—made his own deal at the Devil's Bridge.

According to a swirl of rumors and legends that spread through the city, there was always something mysterious about the bridge on Rose Lane in Mossley, not far from Lennon's childhood home. In one story, a man despondent over a divorce and dire financial conditions traveled to the bridge to kill himself. He left a suicide note, packed his revolver, and walked to the bridge. On the way, maybe to build up some courage, the man stopped at a pub. There, he overheard a bunch of people talking about a soldier who had come back to town, poor and depressed. His wife had abandoned him. However, almost overnight, the soldier had become a wealthy Liverpudlian businessman. Some of the pub revelers had an easy explanation for his sudden change in fortune: the soldier went to the bridge on Rose Lane at midnight and sold his soul.

This man—utterly hopeless—decided to see if there was any truth to the legend. What did he have to lose? He went to the bridge at midnight, just as the soldier in the story had done. At first, nothing happened. Then a dog crossed the bridge, stopped, and barked. The man traced the dog's gaze to a filmy shadow creeping toward him. The figure was more than six feet tall and . . . had horns. So much for the devil appearing in disguise. There was no chitchat; the devil cut to the chase: twenty years of wealth and fortune in exchange for his soul. The man accepted the deal and, according to the legend, lived prosperously for two decades.

And then the devil came back to finish the deal.

Those legends may have circulated around the time Lennon lived in Liverpool. According to one story, Lennon heard the legend and became obsessed with it. He was also obsessed with one single desire: he wanted to be bigger than Elvis. The Beatles, at the time, had been labeled a "bum band" and were considered among the worst in Liverpool. Lennon may have decided that if he wanted to make his rock and roll dream come true, he would need a little help from his friend—or maybe fiend is a better description.

Late one night in December of 1960, the legend goes, Lennon snuck out of his Aunt Mimi's home and went to the bridge on Rose Lane. There, at the stroke of midnight, he met the devil and made his request. The rest is rock and roll history. Lennon and his band, arguably, dethroned the King of Rock and Roll and went on to smash most of Elvis's records. Lennon got his wish: he became bigger than Elvis.

But at what cost?

Some say that his twenty years of fame and fortune ended precisely at the same time that Mark David Chapman shot him as he returned to his apartment in New York City. Believers say this is how the devil collected his final payment on the contract signed at the bridge on Rose Lane.

CHAPTER 37

IF 27 TURNED OUT TO BE 9:

Numerology, Rock and Roll, and the 27 Club

Music is a mathematical language. Notes are frequencies that are divided and then divided again. Harmonies, too, can be described in unique mathematical relationships. Then there is the beat—the foot-stomping, pulsing rhythms that create the hypnotic vibe of rock and roll.

That may be why rock stars seem more superstitious about numbers than any other type of artist. Over the more than half-century of rock and roll history, musicians have stepped forward to reveal their special relationship with numbers.

For numerologists, the number 9 has a special, almost haunted, meaning. The number is a trinity of trinities and is associated with mystics and artists. Maybe that's why this magic number crops up in rock and roll lore. John Lennon referred to the number in the songs "The One After 909," "Revolution 9," and "#9 Dream."

We'll read more about how Lennon was obsessed with the number 9, but it wasn't just the former Beatle who had an affinity with the strange magic of this number.

To get some understanding of the special power of the number, count how often the number 9 turns up in other rock tunes. Jimi Hendrix wrote about it in "If 6 Turned Out to be 9." Keith Richards wrote a tune called "999" for his solo album, and, of course, the Rolling Stones had their own "19th Nervous Breakdown."

There's another way that the number 9 has played a role—a deadly role—in the history of rock and roll. But first, you'll need to understand the weird science of numerology a little better so you can see the connection.

One way numerologists believe you can divine spiritual meaning from numbers is by adding digits together. For instance, if your birthday is on March 10, 1982, or 3/10/1982, then (working backwards) 3+10+1+9+8+2 = 33. Then 3+3 = 6. Your special number, then, is 6. Numerologists then draw up all sorts of attributes for each number that can unlock your destiny. For instance, people whose number is 6 are caring and seek harmony. The numbers also indicate weaknesses that the person should look out for. For example, 6s can come across as intrusive.

It's important to point out that numerology isn't an exact science, nor is it always as simple as the formulas just listed. Each numerologist, it seems, finds a new equation to reveal sacred numbers. They also can come up with new ways to interpret the fortunes based on your numbers, too.

This leads us to the 27 Club, rock and roll's exclusive club for stars who passed away at the age of 27. Numerologists say there may be something about the very digits involved in the number 27 that makes it so interesting, or foreboding—however you choose to think about it. Since the early days of rock and roll, rock stars have seemed to shuffle off the mortal coil soon after they celebrated their 27th birthday. And if you add the 2 and 7 together, you get 9, rock and roll's sacred number. Some numerologists say that 9 represents seers and artists. Is there a better description of rock stars?

Though the 27 Club has an exclusive guest list, the list is pretty extensive, starting with rock's granddaddy. Robert Johnson, the bluesman who is found in the midst of many rock and roll occult tales, is a pioneer once again. He is considered the founding member of the 27 Club. Johnson died at 27, either as a poison victim or as part of a final payment in his deal with the devil.

Brian Jones, one of the founding members of the Rolling Stones, also passed away when he was 27. The guitarist was found floating in his swimming pool. Some blamed drugs, while others suspected foul play. A few other people think the curse of the 27 Club finally caught up with him.

As experimentation with drugs and alcohol became more accepted for rock musicians and other artists, the club got bigger—a lot bigger—in the 1960s. Three of the biggest stars in the 1960s—Jimi Hendrix (died September 18, 1970), Janis Joplin (October 4, 1970), and Jim Morrison (July 3, 1971)—all died before they could reach their 28th birthdays.

Hendrix died in London after a heavy night of drug abuse, although it probably wasn't an exceptional night of binging for the guitar player, who was renowned among rock circles for his ability to ingest vast quantities of drugs and alcohol. When you earn props for your ability to handle booze and drugs from this group of rock and roll animals, it means something. Hendrix, like Lennon, believed that the number 9 dominated his destiny. His birthdate—November 27, 1942—adds up to 9, as pointed out by R. Gary Patterson in his book *Take a Walk on the Dark Side* (11+27+1942 = 1980; 1+9+8 = 18; 1+8 = 9). Hendrix also died at 11:25 p.m. (1+1+2+5 = 9). Hendrix's mother died when she was 27, too. So of all the members of the 27 Club, Jimi seemed to be the most destined to join its ranks.

Drugs were to blame for Janis Joplin's death as well. The singer passed away in a hotel room. Some say the reason she died was because the quality of the heroin was too pure. Usually dealers would slip additives into the heroin to lessen the purity. That way they could make more product with less heroin and make a lot more money. So, sadly, Joplin, who spoke and sang often about being lied to and cheated on, may have died because someone finally didn't cheat her.

Jim Morrison died a poet's death in Paris, slipping under the water while he was taking a bath. There was never an autopsy, but most blamed alcohol as the cause of death. Morrison claimed he was ready to join the club, reportedly telling friends, "You're drinking with number three," in reference to Hendrix and Joplin, the newest 27 Club members.

More of Morrison's 1960s contemporaries would follow. Ron "Pigpen" McKernan was a founding member of the Grateful Dead. As his nickname suggests, Pigpen was not the cleanest guy in the band—a band that, I should emphasize, was never noted for its spiffy, clean image. Most people described Pigpen as a biker with a musician's soul. He played blues organ and harmonica for the band. While most members of the Grateful Dead took a shine to drugs and psychedelics, Pigpen stuck to his biker booze, preferring Thunderbird and Southern Comfort. Pigpen's alcohol abuse was a source of conflict in the band. He was threatened with dismissal—if not outright dismissed, albeit temporarily—on several occasions. Again, let's emphasize: he was getting kicked out of the Grateful Dead for substance abuse. That says a lot.

Grateful or not, in 1973, he became a true member of the dead, joining a long list of rockers who passed away at age 27. The likely cause of death was gastrointestinal hemorrhage brought on by his excessive drinking.

One of Pigpen's singing partners was already a member of the 27 Club when his number was called to join the club. Joplin, who gained fame gigging in the same San Francisco music scene at about the same time that the Grateful Dead was building an audience, joined Pigpen on stage to sing his signature tune, "Turn on Your Lovelight," at the Fillmore West in June of 1969—a moment enshrined in rock and roll history.

In the 1990s, no one epitomized rock and roll rebelliousness like Nirvana guitarist and singer-songwriter Kurt Cobain. Cobain's punk-fueled angst was the driving force in popular music during the '90s. As we mentioned before, the sound that Cobain helped forge in the misty streets of Seattle was named grunge. Lots of critics said that Nirvana and other bands from this Seattle-based music scene helped destroy the hair-band mania that dominated rock and roll in the late 1980s and early 1990s.

And, for that, we should be eternally thankful.

But Cobain was far from thankful, or happy, about his success. When his band became a national, and then global, sensation, he never adjusted to the fame. Even before fame and fortune added increasing pressure to his fragile psyche, the singer had been prone to bouts of depression and self-destruction. Over the years, he developed a serious heroin habit. That habit only accelerated when Cobain had money to indulge it.

Everyone expected the worst.

They might not have known how it would happen, or where it would happen, but those who were familiar with the 27 Club and its open membership to rock stars struggling with inner demons could have guessed how old Cobain would be when he would pledge to the club. So they weren't totally surprised when, on April 5, 1994, entertainment reporters began to spread the sad news that Cobain had been found dead in his home in Lake Washington, Washington.

He was 27.

Cobain allegedly killed himself with a shotgun.

A little over a decade later, a kindred spirit of Cobain's would ask for membership into the club. Amy Winehouse, soul singer and party girl extraordinaire, is one of the most recent members of the 27 Club. She was a lot like Cobain: angry, misunderstood, and extremely addicted. Her membership was somewhat unexpected—only because many people thought she would never even make it to 27.

Winehouse, whose most famous song, "Rehab," dealt with her reluctance to get help with substance abuse, was a shoe-in for the club. Tattooed and troubled, the singer's fights, outbursts, and missed shows were continual fodder for the entertainment media.

People who believe there is an actual 27 Club curse that haunts young rock musicians have even more proof. The members of the club in this chapter are just the well-known rock stars who made the list. There are dozens more who did not. Some never achieved name recognition before they passed on at age 27. Others achieved a cult status in musical genres that are not part of the pop mainstream—musicians like Mia Zapata, member of the Gits who was murdered at 27, and Chris Bell, singer-songwriter for Big Star, a critically acclaimed band that was on the cusp of big-time success.

Another thread ties the members of the 27 Club together: murder.

Most rock historians believe that Robert Johnson was murdered by a jealous lover, or the jealous husband of a lover.

Rumors of foul play have surrounded the deaths of several other members of the 27 Club. There is a rumor that Jimi Hendrix was murdered by a member of his management team. The manager was afraid that Hendrix was preparing to leave the firm—and take his lucrative career elsewhere.

When Brian Jones died, suspicion soon fell on the strange group of hang-abouts who were part of his entourage. Several builders and construction workers with violent reputations were there on the night that Jones drowned. Some believe that they drowned Jones on purpose.

Kurt Cobain's death is also labeled suspicious by rock conspiracy theorists. They believe Cobain didn't commit suicide; they think he was murdered. By whom? The line of suspects is long. Everyone from Cobain's wife, Courtney Love, to greedy drug dealers finds their name on the list of rumored murderers.

Could there be other explanations for the 27 curse?

Skeptics point out that age 27 isn't any more dangerous than any other age for people who partake in high-risk activities, like excessive drug and alcohol use. Some researchers say that the age that these deaths have claimed young artists, while tragic, is just a coincidence.

Adrian Barnett, a researcher at Queensland University of Technology in Australia, did an analysis of the 27 Club. His conclusion was that the age 27 was not significant for rock star deaths, although he did find that rock stars died a lot younger than the average citizen.

There's one problem with the study. The list included musicians who had a number-one hit in the United Kingdom between 1956 and 2007. That rules out stars like Jimi Hendrix, Janis Joplin, and Jim Morrison. However, it did allow in not-so-quintessential rock stars like Frank Sinatra.

This may have significantly edged the curve away from revealing the significance of the 27 Club.

Those who discount the study believe in the curse. They point out that accidents, murder, and other misfortunes have claimed the lives of more than a fair share of 27-year-old rock stars or budding rock stars. In other words, it's not just self-indulgence that leads to membership in the club. Another force appears to be at work.

A mysterious force? Possibly.

The other explanation: it just may be that the contract that these rock stars signed at the crossroads expired when they turned 27.

AFTERWORD
Ghost-Busting the Legends of *Haunted Rock & Roll*

There are believers—people who will believe anything, with or without proof.

There are skeptics—people who demand proof before they believe.

And there are cynics—people who won't believe anything, with or without proof.

As I wrote this and traveled through the Mississippi crossroads and onto the stages where rock and roll was born, and wandered from the darkest depths of the bayou into the big city lights, I managed to become all three—believer, skeptic, and cynic—at one time or another. Sometimes I managed to be all three at once.

Some stories that I collected for this book sound, quite frankly, made up. I would need more evidence or additional testimony to accept some of the tales as anything beyond ghostlore—folklore based on ghosts and apparitions—or practical jokes. Still other stories give me an unsettling feeling that all that we see around us, this solid and apparent world, is not what it seems. I'll get back to that.

But for now, allow me to delve into these stories of rock's biggest haunts to determine, as best as I can, the two questions most of you are asking yourselves: Are these accounts true? And how can you tell the difference?

I'm afraid we won't have any chance of convincing the true cynics that even one story has any basis in reality. But if you are a cynic, I hope this book hasn't been a total waste of time. Even someone who completely doubts the veracity of all these paranormal experiences may be fascinated by why—among all the musical genres and artforms—rock music is so soaked with paranormal lore. To those readers, I recommend that you approach these stories as modern twists on ghostlore—with a backbeat. Ghostlore is a fascinating cultural and literary device that affects your life in ways you may not have considered.

Ghosts have always served as central figures in oral traditions, like folk tales, and in some of the world's most famous literary works. Shakespeare created the ghost of Hamlet's father as a device to show the tenuous balance between sanity and insanity and between reason and intuition. We might consider Hamlet's spirit visitation a form of ghostlore. Tales of murdered brides who haunt forests outside of town and stories of spirits of town founders who haunt mansions are more recent mythological takes on ghostlore. You find these tales in just about every town and every city in the country and around the world.

You can find some of the same elements that define compelling ghostlore—larger-than-life characters, incredible charisma, and outrageous situations—in the legends of rock and roll. Rock music stars are as close to what the ancients called "gods" as our modern culture has.

The late Joseph Campbell, who wrote *The Hero with a Thousand Faces*, a classic text on the relevance of mythology in modern life, discovered the power of rock music—and its ability to inspire myths—after attending a Grateful Dead concert in the mid-1980s.

Although not exactly a fan of rock music, Campbell admitted to feeling rock's power to move people. At a 1986 seminar in San Francisco, he said:

> Rock music has never seemed that interesting to me. It's very simple and the beat is the same old thing. But when you see a room with 8,000 young people for five hours going through it to the beat of these boys ... The genius of these musicians—these three guitars and two wild drummers in the back ... The central guitar, Bob Weir, just controls this crowd and when you see eight thousand kids all going up in the air together ... Listen, this is powerful stuff!

Campbell compared the rock concert to a Dionysian festival, an ancient Greek celebration in honor of the god of fertility and wine:

> This is Dionysus talking through these kids. Now, I've seen similar manifestations, but nothing as innocent as what I saw with this bunch. This was sheer innocence. And when the great beam of light would go over the

> crowd, you'd see these marvelous young faces in sheer rapture—for five hours! Packed together like sardines! Eight thousand of them! Then there was an opening in the back with a series of panel windows and you look out and there's a whole bunch in another hall, dancing crazy. This is a wonderful, fervent loss of self in the larger self of a homogeneous community. This is what it is all about!

Campbell found, as hopefully you did as you read this book, that rock and roll is a perfect stage for modern mythology. He also believed that there are practical purposes for mythology, especially as lessons that can help us better our own lives. Just as we can find guidance in the hijinks and troubles of those mythological gods, so too can we find actual rules for living in some of the rock star ghost stories we covered. Ghost stories can serve as a warning to people who are indulging in harmful activity to stop, and raise the caution flag for those who are considering risky behavior. Experts have found several forms of these cautionary ghost stories in other types of folklore, including urban legends and campus ghostlore. There are corresponding cautionary themes in rock star ghostlore, too. Ghost stories about rock celebrities might be the ultimate warning. Could the haunted tales of Whitney Houston and Jim Morrison help guide people to avoid the same type of self-destructive behaviors that brought down these idols?

Plus, celebrity ghosts add an extra punch to ghostlore because of their power to influence their fans. They star in political ads, promote causes, and raise money for charities. Every time you watch television or read a magazine, some star or model is trying to sell you a product.

So even if all of these stories are nothing more than figments of our imaginations or tales that have been spun into modern morality tales, we can still gain value from rock ghostlore.

If you're a budding ghost hunter or paranormal investigator, the folklore might be interesting, but you're after something much deeper. What if these ghost stories aren't merely twists on urban legends and other manifestations of modern folklore? What if these were real encounters with the supernatural? And, if so, why do rock stars appear in so many ghost stories?

Dan Carlquist, founder and lead investigator of the Ohio Ghost Observers, has been interested in paranormal research for a large portion of his life. He thinks that there could be reasons why celebrities—and especially rock stars—continue to hang around the mortal stage.

"Rock stars, more than most people, love being on stage," Carlquist said in an interview. "They want to feel the adrenaline rush of performing for a crowd."

He says that some spirits are attached to places where they are happiest in life. For rock musicians, that could explain a lot of the hauntings in studios and in the music venues that we reviewed in this book.

"If the theory of spirits being able to spend eternity where they were happiest is true, it makes sense that rock star spirits will be found around clubs, concert halls, and recording studios," Carlquist said. "These spirits want to be seen and heard for as long as possible."

Carlquist has investigated cases in western Pennsylvania and throughout Ohio, including Hill View Manor, Ohio State Reformatory, Prospect Place, Hotel Conneaut, the Bissman Building, and Anna Dean Farm, as well as private homes, hunting cabins, and small businesses. He doesn't believe that all rock star ghost stories are based on legitimate paranormal phenomena, though. Would-be ghost hunters should not stake out the haunted hangouts of their favorite rock stars with preconceived notions, Carlquist advises.

"If you go into a situation hoping to make contact with a particular spirit, you are setting yourself up for failure," he said. "You may think you made contact with something, but in reality you let your imagination get the better of your common sense."

Carlquist investigates all cases looking for ways to debunk them first.

"I am a skeptic first," he added. "It takes a lot for me to say a place has true paranormal activity, and most 'ghosts' can be proven to be nothing more than general home noises and the wind."

His advice for fans who hope to run into their favorite rock idol who has passed on is a bit sobering. Just because you want an encounter doesn't make it any more likely to happen.

"Spirits make contact with individuals on their terms," Carlquist said. "You can ask for a 'sign' until you are blue in the face, but if they don't want to talk, you are out of luck."

Even then, you may not get quite the right reaction from the spirit you're chasing. Do you want the ghost of Jim Morrison, the mellow poet, or the ghost of Jim Morrison, the belligerent drunk?

A final word for those who want to ghost-hunt rock and roll sites: Not all the places listed in this book are public, and not all of the places encourage ghost hunters. Please respect the property rights and privacy rights of these folks by asking for permission before you launch an investigation.

Some places welcome paranormal researchers and even host ghost-hunting tours. Those are the best places to start your own research.

Maybe this is not the most rock and roll way to end this book, but make sure you are responsible and, above all, stay safe.

BIBLIOGRAPHY AND NOTES

Chapter 1

Charters, Samuel B. *Robert Johnson*. Chester, NY: Oak Publications, 1973.

Haunted America Tours. "Robert Johnson's Deal with the Devil and the Crossroads Curse." http://www.hauntedamericatours.com/cursed.

Wolf, Robert. *Hellhound on My Trail: The Life of Robert Johnson, Bluesman Extraordinaire*. Mankato, MN: Creative Editions, 2004.

Chapter 2

Brown, Alan. *Ghosts Along the Mississippi River*. Jackson, MS: University Press of Mississippi, 2011.

———. *Haunted Tennessee: Ghosts and Strange Phenomena of the Volunteer State*. Mechanicsburg, PA: Stackpole Books, 2009.

The Christian Science Monitor. "Elvis Presley: 10 Quotes on His Birthday." http://www.csmonitor.com/Books/2013/0107

/Elvis-Presley-10-quotes-on-his-birthday/You-can-t-hide-from-the-sun.

Cohen, Daniel and Susan. *Hauntings and Horror*. New York: Dutton Juvenile, 2002.

Coleman, Christopher K. *Ghosts and Haunts of Tennessee*. Winston-Salem, NC: John F. Blair, 2011.

Examiner.com "The Ryman Auditorium Is Full of Spirit." http://www.examiner.com/article/the-ryman-auditorium-is-full-of-spirit.

Fire and Ice. "The Charm of Graceland: Gladys Presley and Elvis's Gift of Hospitality and Openness to His Fans." http://fireandice2.blogspot.com/2010/03/charm-of-graceland-gladys-presley-and.html.

Goodreads. Elvis Presley quote. http://www.goodreads.com/quotes/23757-truth-is-like-the-sun-you-can-shut-it-out.

Haunted America Tours. "Elvis' Ghost Has Entered the Building." http://www.hauntedamericatours.com/ghosts/ElvisSeance.php.

Marling, Karal Ann. *Graceland: Going Home with Elvis*. Cambridge, MA: Harvard University Press, 1996.

Paranormal Haze. "Five Celebrity Ghosts." http://www.paranormalhaze.com/5-celebrity-ghosts.

We Must Know. "A Not-So-Superstitious Mind: Elvis Was Obsessed with UFOs." http://wemustknow.wordpress.com/2010/08/26/a-not-so-suspicious-mind-elvis-was-obsessed-with-ufos.

Chapter 3

"Aircraft Accident Report—File No. 2-0001." Civil Aeronautics Board. Page 3, "The Aircraft" section. September 15, 1959. http://data.desmoinesregister.com/holly/documents/CABreport.pdf.

Ghost Traveller. "Iowa Ghosts." http://www.ghosttraveller.com/iowa.htm.

Unexplained Research. "Haunted Milwaukee." Reprint of an article in the *Milwaukee Shepherd Express*, October 27, 2005. http://www.unexplainedresearch.com/media/haunted_milwaukee.html.

Visiting Lindsay Land. "Milwaukee Haunted?" http://lindsaymariepaar.blogspot.com/2005/10/milwaukee-haunted.html.

Chapter 4

Faithfull, Marianne, with David Dalton. *Faithfull: An Autobiography*. New York: Cooper Square Press, 2000.

Patterson, R. Gary. *Take a Walk on the Dark Side*. New York: Fireside, 2004.

Sanchez, Tony. *Up and Down with the Rolling Stones*. London: John Blake, 2011.

Chapter 5

About.com. "Haunted New York City." http://gonyc.about.com/od/halloween/a/haunted_newyork.htm.

The Beatles Browser. Part I, by Bill Harry. http://www.triumphpc.com/mersey-beat/beatles/beatlesbrowser.shtml.

The Beatles Ultimate Experience. David Wigg interview with John Lennon and Yoko Ono on May 8, 1969. http://www.beatlesinterviews.org/db1969.0508.beatles.html.

Cosmic Society of Paranormal Investigation. "Is This John Lennon's Spirit Energy?" http://www.cosmicsociety.com/is_this_john_.htm.

Dead Famous: Ghostly Encounters. "John Lennon." Season 2, Episode 5, 2005. Aired on the Biography Channel.

Exposay. "Liam Gallagher Says He Saw John Lennon's Ghost." http://www.exposay.com/liam-gallagher-says-he-saw-john-lennons-ghost/v/6747. Also reported in the *Daily Star* (UK).

Knoji. "Ghost Story: John Lennon's Ghost Lurks in Obscure Haunted Sightings." http://celebrities.knoji.com/ghost-story-john-lennons-ghost-lurks-in-obscure-haunted-sightings.

O'Hagan, Sean. *The Observer*. "Macca Beyond." September 17, 2005. http://www.guardian.co.uk/music/2005/sep/18/popandrock.paulmccartney.

Ogden, Tom. *Haunted Hollywood: Tinseltown Terrors, Filmdom Phantoms, and Movieland Mayhem*. Guilford, CT: Globe Pequot Press, 2009.

Spitz, Bob. *The Beatles: The Biography*. New York: Little, Brown and Company, 2005.

Tom Slemen (website). "Did John Lennon Sell His Soul?" http://www.slemen.com/lennonsoldsoul.html.

Unexplained Mysteries. "Sir Paul McCartney Haunted by John Lennon's Ghost." http://www.unexplained-mysteries.com/viewnews.php?id=51451.

Chapter 6

Booth, Martin. *A Magick Life: The Life of Aleister Crowley*. London: Coronet Books, 2001.

Case, George. *Jimmy Page: Magus, Musician, Man: An Unauthorized Biography*. New York: Backbeat Books, 2009.

Daily Grail. "Did Aleister Crowley Unleash Demons at Loch Ness?" http://www.dailygrail.com/Magick-Circle/2012/8/Did-Aleister-Crowley-Unleash-Demons-Loch-Ness.

The Great Wen. "Jimmy Page, Aleister Crowley and the Curse of Eddie and the Hot Rods" by Peter Watts. http://greatwen.com/2013/03/27/jimmy-page-aleister-crowley-and-the-curse-of-eddie-and-the-hot-rods.

Herbst, Peter. *The Rolling Stone Interviews.* Page 317. New York: St. Martin's Griffin, 1989.

Herman, Gary. *Rock 'n' Roll Babylon: 50 Years of Sex, Drugs and Rock 'n' Roll.* Medford, NJ: Plexus Publishing, 2007.

Media Underground. "Jimmy Page Talks Magick." December 11, 2007. http://www.media-underground.net/site/index.php?/archives/962-Jimmy-Page-Talks-Magick.html. Excerpt from an interview in *Guitar World* magazine.

Patterson, R. Gary. *Take a Walk on the Dark Side*. New York: Fireside, 2004.

Rolling Stone. "Jimmy Page Once Owned Aleister Crowley's Former Home." http://www.rollingstone.com/music/lists/the-10-wildest-led-zeppelin-legends-fact-checked-20121121/jimmy-page-once-owned-aleister-crowleys-former-home-19691231.

SpookyStuff. "Boleskine House." http://www.spookystuff.co.uk/boleskinehouse.html.

Sutin, Lawrence. *Do What Thou Wilt: A Life of Aleister Crowley*. New York: Griffin Trade Paperbacks, 2002.

Chapter 7

BlogsNRoses. "Exclusive Interview with Otep Shamaya." http://blogsnroses.com/2008/10/31/exclusive-interview-with-otep-shamaya.aspx?ref=rss.

Daily Express. "Researchers Claim Jim Morrison's Ghost Picture Is NOT a Fake." http://www.express.co.uk/news/uk/133169/Researchers-claim-Jim-Morrison-s-ghost-picture-is-NOT-a-fake.

Hollywood Haunts. 2000 Discovery Channel documentary. http://www.nytimes.com/movies/movie/203585/Hollywood-Haunts/overview.

Hopkins, Jerry, and Danny Sugarman. *No One Here Gets Out Alive*. New York: Warner Books, 1995.

Truth Is Scary. Story by AOL News. "Jim Morrison's Ghost Said to Haunt Restaurant Bathroom." http://truthisscary.com/2010/07/jim-morrisons-ghost-said-to-haunt-restaurant-bathroom.

Weidman, Rich. *The Doors FAQ: All That's Left to Know about the Kings of Acid Rock*. Milwaukee, WI: Backbeat Books, 2011. http://books.google.com/books?id=HjPcWkEPSR8C&printsec=frontcover#v=onepage&q&f=false.

Wrap, The. "The Great Ghosts of Rock 'n' Roll." http://www.thewrap.com/blog-entry/great-ghosts-rock-n-roll-9371.

WUSA 9. "Jim Morrison's Spirit Visiting His Old Arlington House?" http://www.wusa9.com/news/article/150732

/373/Jim-Morrisons-Spirit-Visiting-His-Old-Arlington-House.

Chapter 8

BellaOnline. "Janis Joplin Said to Haunt Hotel." http://www.bellaonline.com/articles/art34418.asp.

Fredericksburg.com. "Did Janis Joplin's Ghost Help Transmatic?" http://fredericksburg.com/News/FLS/2002/022002/02282002/534290.

TripAdvisor. Account taken from a review on August 11, 2011, by a guest at the former Albion House Inn. http://www.tripadvisor.com/ShowUserReviews-g60713-d113921-r119650955-Sleep_Over_Sauce-San_Francisco_California.html.

Chapter 9

About.com. "Ghosts of Hollywood Legends, Part 4." http://paranormal.about.com/od/trueghoststories/tp/Ghosts-Of-Hollywood-Legends-4.htm.

Aykroyd, Dan. Huffington Post. "About Ghosts." http://www.huffingtonpost.com/dan-aykroyd/about-ghosts_b_327453.html.

Celebrity Ghost Stories. Featuring Beverly D'Angelo, Season 3, Episode 7. http://www.imdb.com/title/tt1975384.

Real Estalker. "Rent Dan Aykroyd's (Allegedly) Haunted House." http://realestalker.blogspot.com/2007/09/rent-dan-aykroyds-allegedly-haunted.html.

Chapter 10

Billboard. "Park Service Mulls Gram Parsons Memorial." http://www.billboard.com/articles/news/79020/park-service-mulls-gram-parsons-memorial#/news/park-service-mulls-gram-parsons-memorial-964980.story.

Byrd Watcher. "The Strange Death of Gram Parsons: 1973." http://www.ebni.com/byrds/memgrp6.html.

Ghoula. "Legendary Inn for Sale: Spirit & Cat Included." http://ghoula.blogspot.com/2008/01/legendary-inn-for-sale-spirit-cat.html.

Legends of America. "Sleeping With Ghosts in California, Page 3." http://www.legendsofamerica.com/ca-haunted hotels3.html.

New York Times. "A Grievous Angel, A Busy Ghost." December 8, 2002. http://www.nytimes.com/2002/12/08/arts/music-a-grievous-angel-a-busy-ghost.html?pagewanted=all&src=pm.

Chapter 11

Conte, Robert V. *Black Sabbath: The Ozzy Osbourne Years.* Videotape. Studio Chikara, 2000.

Songfacts. Excerpt of *Guitar World* interview with Geezer Butler, July 2001. http://www.songfacts.com/detail.php?id=434.

Taff, Dr. Barry E. *Aliens Above, Ghosts Below.* Harpers Ferry, WV: Cosmic Pantheon Press, 2010. Also based on a follow-up e-mail interview with Dr. Taff.

Chapter 12

Dallas Observer. "Ten Musicians' Ghosts That Still Stalk the Earth (and How to Dress Up as Them for Halloween)." http://blogs.dallasobserver.com/dc9/2011/09/_now_that_the_calendar.php?page=all.

Hittin' the Web with the Allman Brothers Band. "Eddie Hinton, 10 Years Gone ... RIP." Thread on Forum posted on July 25, 2005. http://www.allmanbrothersband.com/modules.php?op=modload&name=XForum&file=viewthread&tid=31700.

Swampland.com. "Richard Young: The Kentucky Headhunters." http://swampland.com/articles/view/title:richard_young_kentucky_headhunters.

Times Daily. "This Is an Article on the Black Keys." http://www.timesdaily.com/archives/article_964a978a-0782-5a52-aba4-56122065cf74.html?mode=story.

Chapter 13

Haunted Places to Go.com. "The Famous Ghosts of the Hotel Chelsea." http://www.haunted-places-to-go.com/famous-ghosts.html.

Living with Legends: Hotel Chelsea Blog. http://www.chelseahotelblog.com/living_with_legends_the_h/ghosts.

USA Today. "Ghosts of Janis, Sid Haunt Chelsea Hotel Film." http://usatoday30.usatoday.com/life/movies/2008-05-25-636874063_x.htm.

Wikiquote. Quote appeared in the *Daily Mirror,* June 11, 1977, as reported on page 197 of Fred and Judy Vermorel's 1987

Sex Pistols: The Inside Story. http://en.wikiquote.org/wiki/Sid_Vicious.

Chapter 14

Brainy Quote. "Kurt Cobain Quotes." http://www.brainyquote.com/quotes/authors/k/kurt_cobain.html.

Haunting Review. "Kurt Cobain: Ghost Box EVP Clips." http://www.hauntingreview.com/kurt-cobain-ghost-box-evp-clips.

Your Ghost Stories. "The Man in the Flannel Shirt." http://www.yourghoststories.com/real-ghost-story.php?story=14731.

Chapter 15

Christian Post. "Michael Jackson's Ghost Allegedly Haunting Neighbors While Celebrities Tweet 'RIP.'" http://global.christianpost.com/news/michael-jacksons-ghost-allegedly-haunting-neighbors-while-celebs-tweet-rip-77175.

CNN. "Michael Jackson's Ghost HQ Edit." http://www.youtube.com/watch?v=zhq9l3c7XgA.

Radar Online. "Ghost of Michael Jackson Tap Dancing in La Toya's Home, She Says." http://radaronline.com/exclusives/2013/04/latoya-jackson-michael-jackson-ghost-tap-dancing.

The Sun. "Jacko's Ghost at Neverland." http://www.thesun.co.uk/sol/homepage/news/2518485/Fans-claim-that-Michael-Jacksons-ghost-has-been-spotted-at-Neverland.html.

Chapter 16

Contactmusic. "Winehouse's Ghost Haunting Pete Doherty's London Home." http://www.contactmusic.com/news/winehouse-ghost-haunting-pete-dohertys-london-home_1260915.

Jezebel. "Bobbi Kristina Is Lovingly Haunted by the Ghost of Whitney Houston." http://jezebel.com/5892396/bobbi-kristina-is-being-lovingly-haunted-by-the-ghost-of-whitney-houston.

Phantoms and Monsters. "Whitney Houston's Distraught Mother Haunted by Her Ghost." http://naturalplaneb-logspot.com/2012/03/esoterica-whitney-houstons-ghost-haunts.html.

Chapter 17

Robert Lang Studios. "The Ghost." http://www.robertlangstudios.com/the-ghost.

The Stranger. "Ghost in the Machine: A Dead Man, Buried Treasure, and the Ghost That Haunts Robert Lang Studio." http://www.thestranger.com/seattle/Content?oid=424480.

Chapter 18

Maxim. "Q&A: Eagle Eye Star Billy Bob Thornton." http://www.maxim.com/movies/qa-eagle-eye-star-billy-bob-thornton.

Chapter 19

FeelNumb.com. "The Red Hot Chili Peppers 'Blood Sugar Sex Magik' Ghost Photo." http://www.feelnumb.com/2009/11/01/red-hot-chili-peppers-blood-sugar-sex-magic-ghost-photo.

Zillow. "Celebrities and Their Haunted Homes." http://www.zillow.com/blog/2010-10-12/celebrities-and-their-haunted-homes.

Chapter 20

About.com. "Ghosts of Memphis." http://memphis.about.com/od/halloween/p/ghosts.htm.

Brown, Alan. *Ghosts Along the Mississippi River*. University Press of Mississippi, 2011.

Ghost Traveller. "Tennessee Haunted Locales." http://www.ghosttraveller.com/tennessee.htm.

Special thanks to paranormal researcher Michael Einspanjer, of Memphis Paranormal Investigations, for all of his insights into the history and haunting of Earnestine and Hazel's.

Chapter 21

Hoosier Paranormal Research. "Mounting Evidence at the Crump Theater Tells Haunting Story." http://hoosierparanormal.com/crump_theater.html.

Midwestern Researchers and Investigators of Paranormal Activity (MRIPA). This group, including the interview with MRIPA founder Jason S. Baker, helped me with the chapter on the Crump. Their website is http://mripa.net.

The group has also posted video evidence from their investigations of the Crump at http://www.youtube.com/watch?v=_bgCdAC6J8E and http://www.youtube.com/watch?v=ATZbAiKE-P8.

Chapter 22

CBS Minnesota. "Minnesota's Most Haunted Places." http://minnesota.cbslocal.com/top-lists/minnesotas-most-haunted-places.

Haunted Houses.com. "First Avenue Night Club." http://www.hauntedhouses.com/states/mn/first_avenue.htm.

JSupernatural Investigators of Minnesota. Case notes from investigation on February 26, 2011. http://www.siminnesota.com/invest_first_avenue.html.

Chapter 23

About.com "Cincinnati Music Hall." http://paranormal.about.com/od/hauntedplaces/ig/Haunted-Theaters/Cincinnati-Music-Hall.htm.

Cincinnati Arts Association. "Guided Ghost Tours of Music Hall." http://www.cincinnatiarts.org/events/detail/ghost-tours.

City Beat. "Cincinnati Music Hall—Ghost Hunt." http://www.citybeat.com/cincinnati/article-19047-cincinnati_music_hall_ghost_hunt.html.

Society for the Preservation of Music Hall. "Engst Letter." http://www.spmhcincinnati.org/documents/Engst-letter-02221987.pdf.

———. "Is Music Hall Haunted?" http://www.spmhcincinnati.org/Music-Hall-History/Haunted-Music-Hall.php.

Chapter 24

Akron Beacon Journal. "Humbard Biography Recalls Tearful Presley." http://www.ohio.com/news/humbard-biography-recalls-tearful-presley-1.66636.

Go Elvis.com. "'Elvis Had a Premonition,' Hairdresser Tells Scholars." http://www.goelvis.com/?p=6.

Humbard, Rex. *The Soul-Winning Century, 1906–2006: The Humbard Family Legacy—100 Years of Ministry*. Dallas, TX: Clarion Call Marketing, 2006.

Larry Geller's Blog. "The Mystery of Jesse Garon." http://www.elvispresleybiography.net/elvis-presley-hairstylist-larry-geller-blog/?p=60.

San Francisco Chronicle. "Clear Vision of Elvis' Final Days." http://www.sfgate.com/style/article/Clear-vision-of-Elvis-final-days-3098780.php#ixzz27xGGbxS5.

67 Not Out. "The Twinless Twin Mystery." http://www.67notout.com/2012/01/twinless-twin-mystery.html.

Chapter 25

98.1 WOGL. "McCartney Reveals Premonition about Beatles' Success, Signs Deal with Mad Men." http://wogl.cbslocal-com/2012/02/16/mccartney-reveals-premonition-about-beatles-success-signs-deal-with-mad-men.

Rare Exception.com. "John's 9: The Relationship Between John Lennon and the Number 9." http://www.rareexception.com/Garden/Beatles/Number9.php.

Squidoo. "Ten Strange Coincidence Examples." http://www.squidoo.com/10-strange-coincidence-examples.

Chapter 26

The Death of Rock: The Archive. "The Buddy Holly Curse." http://www.angelfire.com/music5/archives/curseofholly.html.

Tad Williams (website). "Hearing A New World: The Astral Projections of Joe Meek." http://www.tadwilliams.com/2011/11/hearing-a-new-world-the-astral-projections-of-joe-meek.

Chapter 27

Edgar Cayce's A.R.E. http://www.edgarcayce.org/are/edgarcayce.aspx.

Fairweather Lewis (blog). "Premonitions and Coincidences in the Life of Johnny Horton." http://fairweatherlewis.wordpress.com/2010/05/12/premonitions-and-coincidences-in-the-life-of-johnny-horton.

TopTenz.net. "Top 10 Musicians Who Suddenly Died in the '60s." http://www.toptenz.net/top-10-musicians-who-suddenly-died-in-the-60s.php#1cwvQfFrDJJxfKjA.99.

Chapter 28

Johnstone, Nick. *Patti Smith: A Biography*. London: Omnibus Press, 1997.

Louder Than War. "Patti Smith 'A Biography'—Extracts from the Nick Johnstone–Penned Masterpiece." http:

//louderthanwar.com/patti-smith-a-biography-extracts-from-the-nick-johnstone-penned-masterpiece.

"Scarlet Fever Fantasies." A 1976 *Rolling Stone* interview with Patti Smith accessed at http://www.oceanstar.com/patti/intervus/760101rs.htm.

Chapter 29

Aaron Poehler (blog). "The Strange Case of Bobby Fuller." http://www.aaronpoehler.com/strangecase.html.

Patterson, R. Gary. *Take a Walk on the Dark Side*. New York: Fireside, 2004.

Rock Star Martyr.net. "February 3: The Death Day of Buddy Holly." http://rockstarmartyr.net/february-3-the-death-day-of-buddy-holly.

Secrets in the Wind. "The Buddy Holly 'Curse': Does It Really Exist?" http://secretsinthewind.com/curse.htm.

Chapter 30

About.com. "Ghosts of Hollywood Legends, Part 3." http://paranormal.about.com/od/trueghoststories/tp/Ghosts-Of-Hollywood-Legends-3.htm.

Business Insider. "Eleven Homes That Are Haunted by Celebrities." http://www.businessinsider.com/celebrity-haunted-homes?op=1.

Celebrity Ghost Stories. Season 2, Episode 3. Aired July 31, 2010. http://www.imdb.com/title/tt1691499.

Ogden, Tom. *Haunted Hollywood: Tinseltown Terrors, Filmdom Phantoms, and Movieland Mayhem.* Guilford, CT: Globe Pequot Press, 2009.

Rock Star Martyr.net. "February 3: The Death Day of Buddy Holly." http://rockstarmartyr.net/february-3-the-death-day-of-buddy-holly.

Chapter 31

Case, George. *Jimmy Page: Magus, Musician, Man: An Unauthorized Biography*. New York: Backbeat Books, 2009.

Great Wen, The. "Jimmy Page, Aleister Crowley and the Curse of Eddie and the Hot Rods." http://greatwen.com/2013/03/27/jimmy-page-aleister-crowley-and-the-curse-of-eddie-and-the-hot-rods.

Patterson, R. Gary. *Take a Walk on the Dark Side*. New York: Fireside, 2004.

Chapter 32

The Guardian. "Satan's All-Time Greatest Hit: Will Hodgkinson on the Devil's Interval." http://www.guardian.co.uk/music/2007/oct/12/popandrock.classicalmusicandopera.

Patheos. "The Devil's Interval." http://www.geneveith.com/2011/07/27/the-devils-interval.

Chapter 33

NPR.org. "Jim Sullivan's Mysterious Masterpiece: 'U.F.O.'" http://www.npr.org/2010/12/09/131936448/jim-sullivan-s-mysterious-masterpiece-u-f-o.

Ghost Theory. "UFO: The Disappearance of Musician Jim Sullivan." http://www.ghosttheory.com/2013/01/17/ufo-the-disappearance-of-musician-jim-sullivan.

Chapter 34

Digital Spy. "Brian May Claims 'One Vision' Recording Studio Is 'Cursed.'" http://www.digitalspy.com/music/news/a403274/brian-may-claims-one-vision-recording-studio-is-cursed.html.

Chapter 35

Another Nickel in the Machine. "Mayfair and the Deaths of Harry Nilsson, Mama Cass, and Keith Moon." http://www.nickelinthemachine.com/2008/10/mayfair-and-the-deaths-of-harry-nilsson-mama-cass-and-keith-moon.

The Death of Rock: The Archive. "The Curse of Harry Nilsson." http://www.angelfire.com/music5/archives/curseofnilsson.html.

Chapter 36

Haunted America Tours. "Robert Johnson's Deal with the Devil and the Crossroads Curse." http://www.hauntedamericatours.com/cursed.

Niezgoda, Joseph. *The Lennon Prophecy.* New York: New Chapter Press, 2008.

Slemen.com. Tom Slemen, "Did John Lennon Sell His Soul?" http://www.slemen.com/lennonsoldsoul.html.

Stormloader. "Robert Johnson and the Crossroads Curse." http://crossroads.stormloader.com.

TDBlues. "The Real Crossroads?" http://www.tdblues.com/2008/03/the-real-crossroads.

Unexplained-Mysteries.com. "The Crossroads Demon." Thread on Forum started April 16, 2009. http://www.unexplained-mysteries.com/forums/index.php?showtopic=151798.

Chapter 37

About.com. "How to Calculate Your Numerology Birth Number." http://healing.about.com/od/numerology/a/birth-path-numerology-formula.htm.

BuzzFeed. "The 27 Club: 15 Other Musicians Who Died at Age 27." http://www.buzzfeed.com/daves4/15-other-musicians-who-died-at-age-27.

Numerology.com. "Your Life Path Number." http://www.numerology.com/numerology-news/life-path-number.

Patterson, R. Gary. *Take a Walk on the Dark Side*. New York: Fireside, 2004.

Afterword

Campbell, Joseph. *The Hero with a Thousand Faces*. Third edition. Novato, CA: New World Library, 2008.

Sirbacon.org. "Joseph Campbell and the Grateful Dead." http://www.sirbacon.org/joseph_campbell.htm.

Special thanks to Daniel Carlquist, founder and lead investigator of the Ohio Ghost Observers, www.ohioghostobservers.com, for the interview that makes up the meat of this afterword. There's a hazy area between ghostlore and reported paranormal phenomena. Dan was helpful in separating the two and showing it's possible to be skeptical but not cynical.

StripersOnline. "Joseph Campbell and the Grateful Dead." Joseph Campbell quotes from a seminar at the Palace of Fine Arts, San Francisco, on November 1, 1986. http://www.stripersonline.com/t/575951/joseph-campbell-the-grateful-dead.

To Write to the Author

If you wish to contact the author or would like more information about this book, please write to the author in care of Llewellyn Worldwide Ltd. and we will forward your request. Both the author and publisher appreciate hearing from you and learning of your enjoyment of this book and how it has helped you. Llewellyn Worldwide Ltd. cannot guarantee that every letter written to the author can be answered, but all will be forwarded. Please write to:

Matthew L. Swayne
℅ Llewellyn Worldwide
2143 Wooddale Drive
Woodbury, MN 55125-2989

Please enclose a self-addressed stamped envelope for reply, or $1.00 to cover costs. If outside the U.S.A., enclose an international postal reply coupon.